THE COMPREHENSIVE
MEDITERRANEAN
REFRESH
COOKBOOK FOR BEGINNERS
2024 EDITION

Embark on a 2000 Days Journey of Transformation with Easy, Healthy
and Delicious Recipes Toward a Healthier, Nutritious Lifestyle

Isabelle Dubois

TABLE OF CONTENTS

Chapter 1: Introduction

Origins of The Mediterranean Diet

The Mediterranean diet is rooted in the traditional dietary patterns of the countries bordering the Mediterranean Sea, including Greece, Italy, Spain, and parts of the Middle East and North Africa. The diet gained international recognition and popularity largely due to observations of its health benefits in the mid-20th century.

Origins and Evolution

1. **Ancient Practices:** The Mediterranean diet has ancient roots, with dietary patterns established over thousands of years. The region's diverse cultures have contributed to a rich culinary tapestry, utilizing local ingredients and traditional cooking methods.

2. **Post-World War II Observations:** The diet came into the international spotlight in the 1950s and 1960s when American scientist Ancel Keys observed low incidences of heart disease in the Mediterranean region compared to the United States and Northern Europe. This observation led to the Seven Countries Study, a large-scale research project that further explored the health benefits of the Mediterranean diet.

3. **Role of Agriculture and Geography:** The Mediterranean climate, characterized by hot summers and mild winters, is conducive to growing a variety of fruits, vegetables, grains, and olives. The abundance of these foods led to a diet high in fresh produce, whole grains, and olive oil, with moderate consumption of fish and poultry.

Core Components and Principles

The Mediterranean diet emphasizes:
- A high intake of fruits, vegetables, whole grains, and legumes
- Olive oil as the primary source of fat
- Moderate consumption of fish and poultry
- Limited red meat and dairy products
- Regular, but moderate, wine consumption (particularly red wine)
- A focus on fresh, seasonal, and locally-produced foods
- Social and cultural aspects of eating, including sharing meals with family and friends

Health Benefits and Recognition

Research has consistently shown that the Mediterranean diet is associated with a reduced risk of chronic diseases, including heart disease, stroke, and certain types of cancer. It has also been linked to improved longevity and better quality of life.

In 2010, UNESCO recognized the Mediterranean diet as an Intangible Cultural Heritage of Humanity in Spain, Greece, Italy, and Morocco, acknowledging its cultural significance and its contribution to sustainable and healthy eating.

Modern Adoption

While the diet's popularity has led to increased global adoption, there are concerns about the erosion of traditional dietary patterns in the Mediterranean region itself, due to the influence of Western fast food and processed products. Nonetheless, the Mediterranean diet continues to be held up as a gold standard for healthy eating, emphasizing whole foods, healthy fats, and a balanced approach to nutrition.

In conclusion, the Mediterranean diet is more than just a set of dietary guidelines; it is a holistic approach to eating and living that is deeply rooted in the rich history, agriculture, and culinary traditions of the Mediterranean region. Its emphasis on fresh, wholesome foods and its proven health benefits continue to make it a popular choice for those seeking a healthy and sustainable way of life.

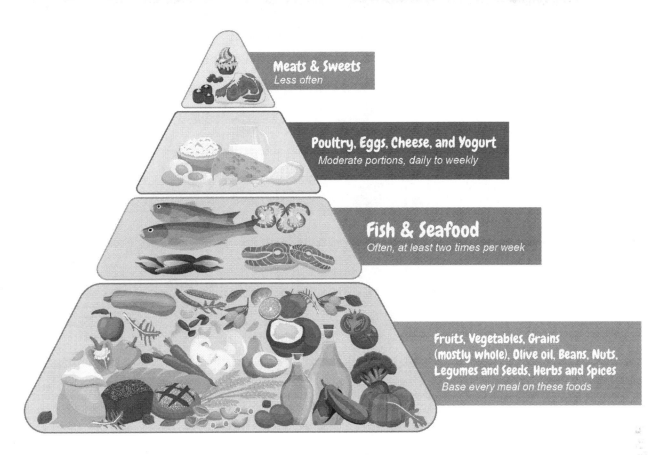

The Mediterranean Diet Pyramid

The Mediterranean Diet Pyramid serves as a guide to help individuals adopt a pattern of eating similar to the traditional diet of the Mediterranean region during the early 1960s. Developed by the Oldways Preservation Trust in collaboration with the Harvard School of Public Health and the WHO in 1993, the pyramid emphasizes a plant-based approach to nutrition, rich in fruits, vegetables, whole grains, and healthy fats.

Base of the Pyramid: Daily Foods

1. **Fruits and Vegetables:** A variety of fruits and vegetables should be consumed in abundance, providing essential vitamins, minerals, and fiber.
2. **Whole Grains:** Foods like whole wheat bread, brown rice, and whole grain pasta should be included in every meal, offering fiber and important nutrients.
3. **Legumes, Nuts, and Seeds:** A good source of protein and healthy fats, these foods should be consumed daily.
4. **Olive Oil:** The primary source of added fat, olive oil is rich in monounsaturated fats and antioxidants.
5. **Herbs and Spices:** Used to flavor foods, reducing the need for salt.

Middle of the Pyramid: Weekly Foods

1. **Fish and Seafood:** Recommended at least twice a week, providing lean protein and omega-3 fatty acids.
2. **Poultry, Eggs, and Dairy:** Moderate portions of poultry and eggs, and daily servings of low-fat dairy products like cheese and yogurt.

Top of the Pyramid: Occasional Foods

1. **Red Meat and Sweets:** Consumed less frequently, red meats are limited, and sweets are saved for special occasions.
2. **Wine:** For those who drink alcohol, wine is included in moderation (one glass per day for women, one to two for men), preferably red wine due to its association with heart health.

Physical Activity and Social Engagement

At the base of the pyramid, physical activity and social engagement are emphasized as integral parts of the diet. Regular physical activity, communal eating, and taking time to savor food are all considered crucial for overall well-being.

Hydration

Water is the recommended beverage of choice, and it should be consumed in abundance throughout the day.

Conclusion

The Mediterranean Diet Pyramid is more than just a food guide; it encompasses a holistic approach to life, encouraging physical activity, mindful eating, and social interactions over meals. It reflects a sustainable way of eating that is not only nutritious but also beneficial for long-term health and well-being.

Health Benefits of The Mediterranean Diet

The Mediterranean diet has been extensively studied for its numerous health benefits. Here's a comprehensive list of the positive impacts it can have on your health:

1. Heart Health

Reduced Risk of Heart Disease: The diet's high content of anti-inflammatory foods and healthy fats, such as olive oil and fish, contribute to a healthier cardiovascular system.

Lower Levels of Bad Cholesterol: The monounsaturated fats in olive oil may help lower "bad" LDL cholesterol levels.

Blood Pressure Control: The inclusion of a variety of fruits and vegetables helps in maintaining healthy blood pressure levels.

2. Weight Management

Supports Healthy Weight: The fiber content in the diet aids in satiety and prevents overeating.

Balanced Macronutrients: The diet provides a balanced mix of carbohydrates, proteins, and fats, helping in maintaining a healthy weight.

3. Brain Health

Cognitive Function: Studies suggest that the Mediterranean diet may improve cognitive function and reduce the risk of Alzheimer's disease.

Mood and Mental Well-Being: The diet is associated with a reduced risk of depression and other mental health disorders.

4. Cancer Prevention

Reduced Cancer Risk: The antioxidants found in fruits, vegetables, and olive oil may contribute to a lower risk of certain types of cancer.

5. Longevity

Increased Lifespan: The diet's rich nutrient profile can contribute to a longer, healthier life.

6. Bone Health

Stronger Bones: The nutrients found in the diet, including calcium from dairy products and vitamin K from leafy greens, support bone health.

7. Diabetes Management

Blood Sugar Control: The diet helps in stabilizing blood sugar levels and has been associated with a reduced risk of type 2 diabetes.

Insulin Sensitivity: The high fiber content and healthy fats can improve insulin sensitivity.

8. Reduced Risk of Stroke

Stroke Prevention: The diet's positive effects on heart health extend to a reduced risk of stroke, particularly in women.

9. Anti-Inflammatory Properties

Fights Inflammation: Many components of the Mediterranean diet have anti-inflammatory properties, reducing the risk of chronic diseases.

10. Better Digestive Health

Digestive Support: The high fiber content aids in digestion and promotes a healthy gut.

11. Skin and Hair Health

Healthy Skin and Hair: The antioxidants and healthy fats in the diet contribute to healthier skin and hair.

12. Sustainable and Eco-Friendly

Positive Environmental Impact: The diet emphasizes plant-based foods, which have a lower environmental footprint than diets high in animal products.

Conclusion

The Mediterranean diet offers a holistic approach to health, promoting physical well-being, mental clarity, and a balanced lifestyle. Its emphasis on fresh, whole foods, along with its numerous health benefits, makes it a sustainable and wise choice for overall health and longevity.

Tips for Adopting a Mediterranean Lifestyle

Adopting a Mediterranean lifestyle goes beyond just the food you eat. It encompasses a broader philosophy that emphasizes simplicity, mindfulness, community, and an appreciation for the joys of life. Here are some tips to help you embrace a Mediterranean lifestyle:

1. Start with Your Plate

- **Prioritize Plant-Based Foods:** Make fruits, vegetables, legumes, nuts, and whole grains the stars of your meals.
- **Choose Healthy Fats:** Replace butter with olive oil. Incorporate sources of omega-3 fats like fish and walnuts.
- **Limit Red Meat:** Opt for poultry or fish as your primary protein sources. If you consume red meat, do so sparingly.
- **Incorporate Dairy:** Consume moderate amounts of cheese and yogurt. Prefer low-fat or non-fat options when possible.
- **Spice It Up:** Use herbs and spices like basil, oregano, and rosemary to add flavor instead of relying on salt.

2. Sip Wisely

- **Hydrate:** Drink plenty of water throughout the day.
- **Limit Sugary Beverages:** Reduce your intake of sodas, sweetened teas, and other high-calorie drinks.
- **Enjoy Wine in Moderation:** If alcohol is appropriate for you, consider having a glass of red wine with meals. Always drink in moderation.

3. Stay Active

- **Daily Movement:** Emphasize daily physical activity, whether it's walking, gardening, dancing, or more structured exercises.
- **Outdoor Activities:** Enjoy nature by hiking, swimming, or even just taking regular walks outside.

4. Connect with Others

- **Share Meals:** In Mediterranean cultures, meals are often a communal event. Share meals with family and friends whenever possible.
- **Foster Community:** Engage in community events, develop strong social connections, and prioritize family.

5. Practice Mindful Eating

- **Savor Each Bite:** Eat slowly, savoring the flavors and textures of your food.
- **Listen to Your Body:** Eat when you're hungry and stop when you're satisfied.

6. Maintain a Balanced Lifestyle

- **Rest and Recover:** Ensure you're getting enough sleep each night.
- **Manage Stress:** Adopt relaxation techniques like meditation, deep breathing exercises, or simply taking time to relax and read.

7. Cook at Home

- **Try New Recipes:** Experiment with traditional Mediterranean recipes.
- **Use Fresh Ingredients:** Prioritize using fresh, seasonal, and locally sourced ingredients.

8. Reduce Processed Foods

- **Read Labels:** Opt for products with recognizable ingredients and avoid those with long lists of additives.
- **Minimize Sugary Treats:** Save desserts and sweets for special occasions.

9. Be Mindful of Portions

Moderation is Key: Even healthy foods should be consumed in moderation. Watch portion sizes to prevent overeating.

10. Appreciate the Simple Joys

Live in the Moment: The Mediterranean lifestyle emphasizes enjoying life's simple pleasures, whether it's the taste of a fresh tomato, the beauty of a sunset, or the joy of good company.

By embracing these principles and incorporating them into your daily life, you'll be well on your way to enjoying the myriad benefits of a Mediterranean lifestyle.

WITHOUT STRESS

Chapter 2: The Basics of Mediterranean Eating

Key Ingredients and Pantry Staples

Embracing the Mediterranean diet involves keeping your kitchen stocked with a variety of healthy and flavorful ingredients. Below is a list of key ingredients and pantry staples commonly used in Mediterranean cuisine:

1. Vegetables

- **Tomatoes:** Fresh or canned, used in salads, sauces, or as a side.
- **Leafy Greens:** Such as spinach, kale, and arugula.
- **Eggplant:** For grilling, roasting, or in stews.
- **Bell Peppers:** Used in a variety of dishes or eaten raw.
- **Zucchini:** Grilled, roasted, or in ratatouille.
- **Garlic:** A base for many Mediterranean recipes.
- **Onions:** Used in sauces, stews, and sautéed dishes.
- **Cucumbers:** Fresh in salads or as a crunchy snack.

2. Fruits

- **Olives:** Green or black, eaten on their own or used to make olive oil.
- **Lemons:** For juicing and zest.
- **Berries:** Fresh or dried.
- **Figs:** Fresh or dried, as a snack or in desserts.
- **Grapes:** Eaten fresh or used to make wine.

3. Proteins

- **Fish:** Such as salmon, sardines, and mackerel.
- **Poultry:** Chicken or turkey.
- **Legumes:** Chickpeas, lentils, and beans.
- **Nuts and Seeds:** Almonds, walnuts, pine nuts, and chia seeds.
- **Cheese:** Feta, halloumi, and Parmesan.
- **Yogurt:** Greek or plain, with no added sugars.

4. Grains

- **Whole Grains:** Brown rice, quinoa, barley, and whole-wheat pasta.
- **Bread:** Whole grain or sourdough.

5. Herbs and Spices

- **Basil:** Fresh or dried.
- **Oregano:** A staple in Greek and Italian dishes.
- **Rosemary:** For roasting and grilling.
- **Thyme:** Adds a fragrant flavor to meats and stews.
- **Parsley:** Fresh for garnishes or in salads.
- **Cumin and Coriander:** For a warm, earthy flavor.
- **Chili Flakes:** To add a bit of heat.

6. Oils and Fats

- **Olive Oil:** Extra virgin for dressings and regular for cooking.
- **Olives:** Various types for snacks or to add to dishes.

7. Pantry Staples

- **Canned Tomatoes:** For sauces and stews.
- **Canned or Dried Beans:** For protein in salads or mains.
- **Whole Wheat Flour:** For baking and coating.
- **Vinegars:** Such as red wine vinegar or balsamic for dressings.

8. Dairy

- **Greek Yogurt:** For breakfast or as a base for sauces.
- **Feta Cheese:** Crumbly and salty, perfect for salads.
- **Parmesan Cheese:** Grated over pasta and salads.

9. Seafood

- **Fish:** Especially fatty fish like salmon, mackerel, and sardines.
- **Shellfish:** Such as shrimp, mussels, and clams.

By keeping these items on hand, you'll be able to whip up a variety of Mediterranean-inspired dishes, benefiting from both their nutritional value and their delicious flavors. Remember to focus on whole, minimally processed foods for the greatest health benefits.

Essential Kitchen Tools and Equipment

When preparing Mediterranean cuisine, having the right kitchen tools and equipment can make the cooking process smoother and more enjoyable. Below is a list of essential kitchen tools and equipment that can help you create delicious and healthy Mediterranean dishes:

1. Knives and Cutting Tools:

- **Chef's Knife:** For chopping, dicing, and mincing a variety of ingredients.
- **Paring Knife:** For peeling and slicing smaller fruits and vegetables.
- **Bread Knife:** Ideal for slicing through crusty breads.
- **Cutting Board:** Preferably wood or bamboo.

2. Cookware:

- **Skillet or Frying Pan:** For sautéing vegetables, cooking meats, and making sauces.
- **Saucepan:** For cooking grains, making sauces, and boiling vegetables.
- **Stock Pot:** For making soups and stews.
- **Grill Pan or Outdoor Grill:** For grilling meats, vegetables, and seafood.
- **Baking Dish:** For roasting vegetables and baking casseroles.
- **Roasting Pan:** For cooking larger cuts of meat or poultry.

3. Bakeware:

- **Sheet Pan:** For roasting vegetables and baking.
- **Loaf Pan:** For baking breads.
- **Mixing Bowls:** In various sizes for prep work and mixing.

4. Utensils:

- **Spatula:** For flipping and stirring.
- **Ladle:** For serving soups and stews.
- **Whisk:** For mixing dressings and sauces.
- **Tongs:** For turning meats and vegetables on the grill or in the pan.
- **Vegetable Peeler:** For peeling fruits and vegetables.
- **Grater:** For grating cheese and vegetables.
- **Mortar and Pestle or Spice Grinder:** For grinding spices and making pastes.

5. Appliances:

- **Food Processor:** For chopping, slicing, and making sauces and dips.
- **Blender:** For making smoothies, soups, and sauces.
- **Grill or Panini Press:** For grilling sandwiches and meats.

6. Miscellaneous:

- **Olive Oil Dispenser:** For easily adding olive oil to dishes.
- **Citrus Juicer or Reamer:** For juicing lemons and other citrus fruits.
- **Garlic Press:** For easily mincing garlic.
- **Herb Scissors or Herb Stripper:** For easily cutting fresh herbs.
- **Measuring Cups and Spoons:** For accurate ingredient measurements.
- **Salad Spinner:** For cleaning and drying leafy greens.
- **Colander or Strainer:** For draining pasta and rinsing vegetables.

Having these tools on hand will help you prepare a variety of Mediterranean recipes with ease, from simple salads and grilled vegetables to complex stews and baked dishes. Remember to maintain your tools well, keeping knives sharp and appliances clean, to ensure they are always ready for use.

Cooking Techniques and Tips

Adopting Mediterranean cooking techniques and tips can enhance the flavors in your food while also supporting a healthy lifestyle. Here's a guide to some essential techniques and tips used in Mediterranean cooking:

Cooking Techniques

- **Grilling:** One of the most popular Mediterranean cooking methods. Grill vegetables, fish, and lean meats to add a smoky flavor.
- **Roasting:** Roast vegetables and meats at a high temperature to caramelize the outside while keeping the inside moist.
- **Sautéing:** Use a small amount of olive oil to quickly cook vegetables or meats over medium-high heat.
- **Braising:** Slow cook meats and vegetables in a small amount of liquid to tenderize and enhance flavors.
- **Baking:** Utilize the oven for baking fish, poultry, bread, and pastries.
- **Poaching:** Gently simmer ingredients in liquid until cooked through. This works well for fish and eggs.
- **Steaming:** Preserve nutrients in vegetables by steaming them until just tender.

Preparation Tips:

- **Use Fresh Ingredients:** Opt for fresh, seasonal produce, and high-quality meats and seafood.
- **Incorporate Herbs and Spices:** Enhance flavors with a variety of herbs and spices like garlic, oregano, rosemary, and basil.
- **Embrace Healthy Fats:** Utilize sources of healthy fats, such as olive oil, nuts, and avocados.
- **Whole Grains:** Incorporate whole grains like quinoa, farro, and brown rice into your meals.
- **Legumes and Beans:** Add lentils, chickpeas, and beans as protein sources and for added fiber.

Cooking Tips:

- **Moderation with Oil:** While olive oil is healthy, it is also calorie-dense. Use it sparingly to sauté or dress salads.
- **Slow Cook Flavors:** Allow stews and sauces to simmer for longer periods to develop deeper flavors.
- **Balance Your Plate:** Aim for a balanced plate with a variety of food groups, focusing on vegetables, whole grains, and lean proteins.
- **Prep in Advance:** Prep ingredients in advance to make cooking through the week quicker and easier.
- **Cook in Batches:** Prepare and cook large batches of meals to have leftovers for the week or to freeze for later use.
- **Taste as You Go:** Adjust seasonings as you cook to suit your taste preferences.
- **Use Citrus:** Brighten up dishes with a squeeze of fresh lemon or orange juice.
- **Don't Overcook Vegetables:** Cook vegetables until just tender to preserve nutrients and texture.
- **Practice Portion Control:** Pay attention to portion sizes, especially with higher calorie foods like nuts and oils.
- **Stay Hydrated:** Drink plenty of water throughout the day, and enjoy wine in moderation.

By incorporating these techniques and tips into your cooking routine, you can create flavorful and nutritious meals that align with the Mediterranean diet and lifestyle.

Chapter 3: Breakfast

Greek Yogurt Parfait with Fresh Berries and Honey

Prep: 10 mins | Serves: 2

Ingredients:
- 2 cups Greek yogurt
- 1 cup mixed fresh berries (strawberries, blueberries, raspberries)
- 2 tablespoons honey
- 1/4 cup granola
- Fresh mint leaves for garnish (optional)

Instructions:
1. In two serving glasses or bowls, start by layering 1/4 cup of Greek yogurt at the bottom.
2. Add a layer of mixed fresh berries on top of the yogurt.
3. Drizzle a tablespoon of honey over the berries.
4. Repeat the layers until the glasses are filled, finishing with a layer of berries on top.
5. Top each parfait with a sprinkle of granola and garnish with fresh mint leaves if using.
6. Serve immediately or refrigerate until ready to serve.

Nutrition Facts: Calories: 210 | Fat: 2g | Protein: 20g | Carbohydrates: 30g | Fiber: 4g

Mediterranean Vegetable Omelette

Prep: 10 mins | Cook: 10 mins | Serves: 1

Ingredients:
- 2 large eggs
- Salt and pepper to taste
- 1 tablespoon olive oil
- 1/4 cup diced red bell pepper
- 1/4 cup diced zucchini
- 1/4 cup cherry tomatoes, halved
- 1 tablespoon chopped olives
- 1 tablespoon crumbled feta cheese
- Fresh basil leaves for garnish

Instructions:
1. In a bowl, whisk the eggs with salt and pepper until well beaten.
2. Heat the olive oil in a non-stick skillet over medium heat.
3. Add the diced red bell pepper and zucchini, and sauté for 3-4 minutes until they start to soften.
4. Add the cherry tomatoes and olives, and continue to sauté for another 2 minutes.
5. Pour the beaten eggs over the vegetables, tilting the pan to spread them evenly.
6. Cook for 2-3 minutes, until the edges start to set.
7. Sprinkle the feta cheese over one half of the omelette.
8. Using a spatula, fold the other half over the cheese.
9. Cook for another 1-2 minutes, until the omelette is fully set and the cheese has melted.
10. Slide the omelette onto a plate, garnish with fresh basil, and serve immediately.

Nutrition Facts: Calories: 350 | Fat: 27g | Protein: 19g | Carbohydrates: 10g | Fiber: 2g

Spinach and Feta Scramble

Prep: 5 mins | Cook: 5 mins | Serves: 1

Ingredients:
- 2 large eggs
- Salt and pepper to taste
- 1 tablespoon olive oil
- 1 cup fresh spinach leaves
- 1/4 cup crumbled feta cheese
- Fresh dill for garnish (optional)

Instructions:
1. In a bowl, whisk the eggs with salt and pepper until well beaten.
2. Heat the olive oil in a non-stick skillet over medium heat.
3. Add the spinach leaves and sauté for 1-2 minutes until wilted.
4. Pour the beaten eggs over the spinach.
5. Allow the eggs to set for a few seconds, then gently scramble until they are fully cooked but still soft.
6. Sprinkle the feta cheese over the scrambled eggs.
7. Cook for an additional 30 seconds until the cheese is slightly melted.
8. Transfer the scramble to a plate, garnish with fresh dill if using, and serve immediately.

Nutrition Facts: Calories: 290 | Fat: 23g | Protein: 16g | Carbohydrates: 4g | Fiber: 1g

Avocado Toast with Tomato and Basil

Prep: 5 mins | Cook: 5 mins | Serves: 1

Ingredients:
- 1 slice whole grain bread
- 1/2 ripe avocado
- 1/4 cup cherry tomatoes, halved
- Fresh basil leaves
- Salt and pepper to taste
- Drizzle of olive oil (optional)

Instructions:
1. Toast the bread slice to your liking.
2. While the bread is toasting, mash the avocado in a bowl and season with salt and pepper.
3. Spread the mashed avocado evenly over the toasted bread.
4. Top with cherry tomato halves and fresh basil leaves.
5. If desired, finish with a drizzle of olive oil.
6. Serve immediately.

Nutrition Facts: Calories: 280 | Fat: 15g | Protein: 7g | Carbohydrates: 30g | Fiber: 7g

Shakshuka with Bell Peppers and Feta

Prep: 10 mins | Cook: 30 mins | Serves: 4

Ingredients:
- 2 tablespoons olive oil
- 1 onion, diced
- 1 red bell pepper, diced
- 3 garlic cloves, minced
- 1 teaspoon ground cumin
- 1 teaspoon paprika
- 1/2 teaspoon cayenne pepper (adjust to taste)
- 1 can (28 oz) crushed tomatoes
- Salt and pepper to taste
- 4-6 large eggs
- 1/2 cup crumbled feta cheese
- Fresh parsley for garnish

Instructions:
1. Heat the olive oil in a large skillet over medium heat.
2. Add the onion and bell pepper, and cook for 5-7 minutes until softened.
3. Add the garlic, cumin, paprika, and cayenne pepper, and cook for another 1-2 minutes until fragrant.
4. Pour in the crushed tomatoes, season with salt and pepper, and stir well.
5. Bring the mixture to a simmer, reduce the heat to low, and cook for 10-15 minutes until it thickens slightly.
6. Create wells in the sauce with a spoon, and crack the eggs into each well.
7. Cover the skillet and cook for 5-7 minutes, or until the eggs are done to your liking.
8. Sprinkle the feta cheese over the top.
9. Garnish with fresh parsley, and serve straight from the skillet with crusty bread on the side.

Nutrition Facts: Calories: 320 | Fat: 20g | Protein: 14g | Carbohydrates: 20g | Fiber: 5g

Olive Tapenade on Whole Grain Toast

Prep: 10 mins | Cook: 2 mins | Serves: 2

Ingredients:
- 4 slices whole grain bread
- 1 cup mixed olives, pitted
- 2 tablespoons capers
- 2 garlic cloves
- Juice of 1 lemon
- 2 tablespoons olive oil
- Fresh parsley, chopped (for garnish)
- Salt and pepper to taste

Instructions:
1. Place the olives, capers, garlic, lemon juice, and olive oil in a food processor.
2. Pulse until the ingredients are finely chopped but not puréed, maintaining a bit of texture.
3. Toast the whole grain bread slices to your liking.
4. Spread a generous amount of olive tapenade on each slice of toast.
5. Season with salt and pepper to taste, and garnish with chopped fresh parsley.
6. Serve immediately and enjoy!

Nutrition Facts: Calories: 220 | Fat: 12g | Protein: 6g | Carbohydrates: 22g | Fiber: 4g

Quinoa Breakfast Bowl with Fruit and Nuts

Prep: 5 mins | Cook: 15 mins | Serves: 2

Ingredients:
- 1 cup quinoa, rinsed
- 2 cups almond milk
- 1 cinnamon stick
- 1 apple, diced
- 1 banana, sliced
- 1/4 cup mixed nuts (almonds, walnuts, pecans), chopped
- 2 tablespoons honey or maple syrup
- Fresh berries for garnish

Instructions:
1. In a medium saucepan, combine the quinoa, almond milk, and cinnamon stick.
2. Bring to a boil, then reduce heat to low, cover, and simmer for 15 minutes, or until quinoa is cooked and liquid is absorbed.
3. Remove from heat and let it sit for 5 minutes, then fluff with a fork and remove the cinnamon stick.
4. Divide the cooked quinoa between two bowls.
5. Top with diced apple, banana slices, chopped nuts, and a drizzle of honey or maple syrup.
6. Garnish with fresh berries and serve immediately.

Nutrition Facts: Calories: 380 | Fat: 12g | Protein: 10g | Carbohydrates: 60g | Fiber: 8g

Almond and Apricot Overnight Oats
Prep: 5 mins | Serves: 1

Ingredients:
- 1/2 cup rolled oats
- 3/4 cup almond milk
- 1/4 cup dried apricots, chopped
- 2 tablespoons almond slivers
- 1 tablespoon chia seeds
- 1 tablespoon honey or maple syrup
- 1/2 teaspoon vanilla extract

Instructions:
1. In a jar or airtight container, combine all ingredients.
2. Stir well to ensure that the oats are fully submerged in the almond milk.
3. Seal the container and refrigerate overnight (or for at least 6 hours).
4. When ready to eat, give the oats a good stir, and add a splash of almond milk if needed to reach your desired consistency.
5. Serve cold or at room temperature, and enjoy!

Nutrition Facts: Calories: 320 | Fat: 9g | Protein: 9g | Carbohydrates: 50g | Fiber: 8g

Mediterranean Breakfast Tacos with Hummus

Prep: 10 mins | Cook: 10 mins | Serves: 2

Ingredients:
- 4 small whole wheat tortillas
- 1 cup hummus (store-bought or homemade)
- 1 cup cherry tomatoes, halved
- 1 cucumber, diced
- 1/4 red onion, thinly sliced
- 1/4 cup crumbled feta cheese
- 1 tablespoon olive oil
- Juice of 1 lemon
- Fresh parsley, chopped (for garnish)
- Salt and pepper to taste

Instructions:
1. In a skillet over medium heat, warm the whole wheat tortillas for about 30 seconds on each side, or until they are soft and pliable.
2. Spread a generous layer of hummus on each tortilla.
3. Top with cherry tomatoes, cucumber, red onion, and crumbled feta cheese.
4. Drizzle with olive oil and a squeeze of fresh lemon juice.
5. Season with salt and pepper to taste, and garnish with chopped fresh parsley.
6. Fold the tortillas in half to form tacos, and serve immediately.

Nutrition Facts: Calories: 320 | Fat: 16g | Protein: 12g | Carbohydrates: 35g | Fiber: 6g

Fig and Walnut Yogurt Bowl

Prep: 5 mins | Serves: 1

Ingredients:
- 1 cup Greek yogurt
- 5-6 fresh figs, quartered
- 1/4 cup walnuts, chopped
- 1 tablespoon honey or maple syrup
- A pinch of cinnamon

Instructions:
1. Place the Greek yogurt in a bowl.
2. Arrange the fresh fig quarters on top of the yogurt.
3. Sprinkle with chopped walnuts.
4. Drizzle with honey or maple syrup, and add a pinch of cinnamon.
5. Serve immediately and enjoy your nutritious breakfast!

Nutrition Facts: Calories: 420 | Fat: 20g | Protein: 25g | Carbohydrates: 40g | Fiber: 6g

Baked Eggs with Spinach and Olives

Prep: 10 mins | Cook: 15 mins | Serves: 2

Ingredients:
- 4 large eggs
- 2 cups fresh spinach
- 1/2 cup black olives, pitted and sliced
- 1/4 red onion, thinly sliced
- 2 cloves garlic, minced
- 1 tablespoon olive oil
- Salt and pepper to taste
- Fresh parsley for garnish (optional)

Instructions:
1. Preheat your oven to 375°F (190°C).
2. In a skillet over medium heat, add the olive oil, garlic, and red onion. Sauté for 2-3 minutes until the onion is softened.
3. Add the spinach and cook for an additional 2 minutes until the spinach is wilted.
4. Stir in the sliced olives and season with salt and pepper.
5. Divide the spinach and olive mixture between two oven-safe dishes.
6. Make two wells in each dish and crack two eggs into each.
7. Place the dishes in the preheated oven and bake for 10-12 minutes, or until the eggs are set to your liking.
8. Remove from the oven, garnish with fresh parsley if using, and serve immediately.

Nutrition Facts: Calories: 220 | Fat: 15g | Protein: 13g | Carbohydrates: 6g | Fiber: 2g

Zucchini and Feta Pancakes

Prep: 15 mins | Cook: 10 mins | Serves: 4

Ingredients:
- 2 medium zucchinis, grated
- 1/2 cup crumbled feta cheese
- 2 large eggs
- 1/4 cup all-purpose flour
- 2 green onions, finely chopped
- Salt and pepper to taste
- Olive oil for frying

Instructions:
1. Place the grated zucchini in a clean kitchen towel and squeeze out as much liquid as possible.
2. In a bowl, combine the zucchini, feta cheese, eggs, flour, green onions, salt, and pepper.
3. Mix until well combined.
4. Heat a bit of olive oil in a skillet over medium heat.
5. Spoon the zucchini mixture into the skillet, forming small pancakes.
6. Cook for 3-4 minutes on each side, or until golden brown and cooked through.
7. Remove from the skillet and serve immediately.

Nutrition Facts: Calories: 170 | Fat: 10g | Protein: 9g | Carbohydrates: 12g | Fiber: 2g

Smoked Salmon and Avocado Toast

Prep: 10 mins | Cook: 5 mins | Serves: 2

Ingredients:
- 4 slices whole grain bread
- 4 ounces smoked salmon
- 1 ripe avocado, sliced
- 1 tablespoon capers
- 1 tablespoon fresh dill, chopped
- Juice of 1 lemon
- Salt and pepper to taste

Instructions:
1. Toast the bread slices to your liking.
2. Spread the avocado slices evenly over the toasted bread.
3. Top with smoked salmon, capers, and chopped dill.
4. Squeeze a bit of fresh lemon juice over each slice.
5. Season with salt and pepper to taste.
6. Serve immediately and enjoy!

Nutrition Facts: Calories: 300 | Fat: 15g | Protein: 15g | Carbohydrates: 25g | Fiber: 5g

Tomato and Cucumber Salad with Pita

Prep: 10 mins | Serves: 4

Ingredients:
- 4 medium tomatoes, diced
- 1 large cucumber, diced
- 1/4 red onion, thinly sliced
- 1/4 cup fresh parsley, chopped
- 1/4 cup olive oil
- Juice of 1 lemon
- Salt and pepper to taste
- 4 pita breads, warmed

Instructions:
1. In a large bowl, combine the diced tomatoes, diced cucumber, sliced red onion, and chopped parsley.
2. Drizzle with olive oil and lemon juice, and season with salt and pepper.
3. Toss well to combine.
4. Serve immediately with warmed pita bread on the side.

Nutrition Facts: Calories: 250 | Fat: 14g | Protein: 5g | Carbohydrates: 30g | Fiber: 4g

Berry and Chia Seed Smoothie

Prep: 5 mins | Serves: 2

Ingredients:
- 1 cup mixed berries (strawberries, blueberries, raspberries, blackberries)
- 1 banana
- 2 tablespoons chia seeds
- 1 cup Greek yogurt
- 1 cup almond milk
- 1 tablespoon honey or maple syrup

Instructions:
1. In a blender, combine the mixed berries, banana, chia seeds, Greek yogurt, almond milk, and honey or maple syrup.
2. Blend until smooth.
3. Pour into glasses and serve immediately.

Nutrition Facts: Calories: 250 | Fat: 6g | Protein: 10g | Carbohydrates: 40g | Fiber: 7g

Poached Eggs with Yogurt and Spicy Butter

Prep: 10 mins | Cook: 10 mins | Serves: 2

Ingredients:
- 4 large eggs
- 1 cup Greek yogurt
- 2 tablespoons unsalted butter
- 1 teaspoon paprika
- 1/2 teaspoon cayenne pepper
- 2 cloves garlic, minced
- Salt to taste
- Fresh parsley for garnish

Instructions:
1. Fill a large pot with water and bring to a simmer.
2. In a small bowl, whisk the Greek yogurt until smooth, and divide between two plates.
3. In a small saucepan, melt the butter over medium heat. Add the paprika, cayenne pepper, and minced garlic. Stir well and cook for 1-2 minutes until fragrant. Remove from heat.
4. Crack each egg into a small bowl. Create a gentle whirlpool in the water and slowly tip the egg into the center. Poach for 3-4 minutes or until the whites are set but the yolks remain runny. Use a slotted spoon to remove the eggs and place them on top of the yogurt.
5. Drizzle the spicy butter over the eggs and yogurt.
6. Season with salt to taste and garnish with fresh parsley.
7. Serve immediately and enjoy!

Nutrition Facts: Calories: 350 | Fat: 25g | Protein: 18g | Carbohydrates: 10g | Fiber: 0g

Mediterranean Breakfast Burrito

Prep: 15 mins | Cook: 10 mins | Serves: 2

Ingredients:
- 2 whole wheat tortillas
- 4 large eggs, beaten
- 1/2 cup black beans, drained and rinsed
- 1/2 avocado, sliced
- 1/2 cup cherry tomatoes, halved
- 1/4 red onion, finely chopped
- 1/4 cup feta cheese, crumbled
- 1 tablespoon olive oil
- Salt and pepper to taste
- Fresh cilantro for garnish

Instructions:
1. In a skillet, heat the olive oil over medium heat. Add

the beaten eggs, salt, and pepper. Scramble until just set.
2. Warm the tortillas in a dry skillet or in the microwave for 15-20 seconds.
3. Divide the scrambled eggs between the two tortillas.
4. Top with black beans, avocado slices, cherry tomatoes, red onion, and feta cheese.
5. Roll up the burritos, tucking in the sides as you go.
6. Serve immediately, garnished with fresh cilantro.

Nutrition Facts: Calories: 450 | Fat: 22g | Protein: 20g | Carbohydrates: 40g | Fiber: 7g

Greek Honey and Nut Porridge

Prep: 5 mins | Cook: 10 mins | Serves: 2

Ingredients:
• 1 cup rolled oats
• 2 cups milk (dairy or plant-based)
• 1/4 cup honey
• 1/2 teaspoon cinnamon
• 1/4 cup walnuts, chopped
• 1/4 cup almonds, chopped
• 2 tablespoons raisins or sultanas
• Fresh fruits for garnish

Instructions:
1. In a saucepan, bring the milk to a boil. Add the oats and reduce the heat to simmer, stirring occasionally, until the oats are cooked and creamy.
2. Stir in the honey and cinnamon.
3. Divide the porridge between two bowls.
4. Top with chopped walnuts, almonds, and raisins or sultanas.
5. Garnish with fresh fruits of your choice.
6. Serve immediately and enjoy!

Nutrition Facts: Calories: 350 | Fat: 12g | Protein: 10g | Carbohydrates: 50g | Fiber: 6g

Caprese Avocado Toast

Prep: 5 mins | Cook: 5 mins | Serves: 2

Ingredients:
• 4 slices whole grain bread
• 1 ripe avocado, mashed
• 1 medium tomato, sliced
• 1/2 ball fresh mozzarella cheese, sliced
• Fresh basil leaves
• Balsamic glaze for drizzling
• Salt and pepper to taste

Instructions:
1. Toast the bread slices to your liking.
2. Spread the mashed avocado evenly over each slice.
3. Top with slices of tomato and mozzarella cheese.
4. Season with salt and pepper.
5. Garnish with fresh basil leaves.
6. Drizzle with balsamic glaze.
7. Serve immediately and enjoy!

Nutrition Facts: Calories: 320 | Fat: 16g | Protein: 12g | Carbohydrates: 30g | Fiber: 7g

Spinach and Mushroom Frittata

Prep: 10 mins | Cook: 20 mins | Serves: 4

Ingredients:
• 6 large eggs
• 2 cups fresh spinach, chopped
• 1 cup mushrooms, sliced
• 1/2 onion, diced
• 2 cloves garlic, minced
• 1/4 cup milk
• 1/2 cup grated Parmesan cheese
• 2 tablespoons olive oil
• Salt and pepper to taste

Instructions:
1. Preheat your oven to 375°F (190°C).
2. In a bowl, whisk together the eggs, milk, Parmesan cheese, salt, and pepper.
3. In an oven-safe skillet, heat the olive oil over medium heat. Add the onions and garlic, and sauté until the onions are translucent.
4. Add the mushrooms and cook for another 3-4 minutes.
5. Stir in the chopped spinach and cook until just wilted.
6. Pour the egg mixture over the vegetables, making sure the ingredients are evenly distributed.
7. Cook for 2-3 minutes until the edges start to set, then transfer the skillet to the preheated oven.
8. Bake for 15-20 minutes, or until the frittata is set and slightly golden on top.
9. Remove from the oven and let it cool for a few minutes before slicing and serving.

Nutrition Facts: Calories: 220 | Fat: 14g | Protein: 15g | Carbohydrates: 8g | Fiber: 2g

Eggplant and Tomato Shakshuka

Prep: 15 mins | Cook: 25 mins | Serves: 4

Ingredients:
• 1 large eggplant, diced
• 1 can (28 oz) diced tomatoes
• 1 onion, chopped
• 3 cloves garlic, minced
• 4 large eggs
• 2 tablespoons olive oil
• 1 teaspoon cumin
• 1 teaspoon paprika
• 1/2 teaspoon chili flakes (optional)
• Salt and pepper to taste
• Fresh cilantro or parsley for garnish

Instructions:
1. Heat the olive oil in a large skillet over medium heat. Add the eggplant, onion, and garlic. Sauté until the vegetables are softened, about 7-10 minutes.
2. Add the diced tomatoes, cumin, paprika, chili flakes (if using), salt, and pepper. Stir well and let the mixture simmer for 10-12 minutes until it thickens slightly.
3. Create four wells in the tomato-eggplant mixture and crack an egg into each well.
4. Cover the skillet and let it cook for 5-7 minutes or until the eggs are cooked to your liking.

5. Garnish with fresh cilantro or parsley.
6. Serve immediately with crusty bread or pita.

Nutrition Facts: Calories: 220 | Fat: 12g | Protein: 10g | Carbohydrates: 20g | Fiber: 6g

Lemon and Poppy Seed Greek Yogurt Pancakes

Prep: 10 mins | Cook: 15 mins | Serves: 4

Ingredients:
- 1 1/2 cups all-purpose flour
- 2 teaspoons baking powder
- 1/2 teaspoon baking soda
- 2 tablespoons sugar
- 2 tablespoons poppy seeds
- Zest of 1 lemon
- 1 cup Greek yogurt
- 1/2 cup milk
- 2 large eggs
- 2 tablespoons melted butter
- 1 teaspoon vanilla extract

Instructions:
1. In a large bowl, combine the flour, baking powder, baking soda, sugar, poppy seeds, and lemon zest.
2. In another bowl, mix together the Greek yogurt, milk, eggs, melted butter, and vanilla extract.
3. Add the wet ingredients to the dry ingredients, stirring just until combined.
4. Preheat a skillet or griddle over medium heat and lightly grease it.
5. Pour 1/4 cup of batter onto the skillet for each pancake. Cook until bubbles form on the surface, then flip and cook until golden brown on the other side.
6. Serve with lemon wedges and maple syrup.

Nutrition Facts: Calories: 290 | Fat: 9g | Protein: 12g | Carbohydrates: 40g | Fiber: 2g

Breakfast Couscous with Dried Fruit

Prep: 5 mins | Cook: 10 mins | Serves: 4

Ingredients:
- 1 cup couscous
- 1 1/2 cups milk (dairy or plant-based)
- 1/4 cup dried apricots, chopped
- 1/4 cup raisins or sultanas
- 2 tablespoons honey or maple syrup
- 1/2 teaspoon cinnamon
- 1/4 cup almonds, chopped
- Fresh mint for garnish

Instructions:
1. In a saucepan, bring the milk to a boil.
2. Stir in the couscous, dried apricots, and raisins or sultanas. Cover and remove from heat. Let it sit for 5 minutes.
3. Fluff the couscous with a fork and stir in the honey or maple syrup, and cinnamon.
4. Divide the couscous between bowls, and top with chopped almonds.
5. Garnish with fresh mint.
6. Serve warm and enjoy!

Nutrition Facts: Calories: 250 | Fat: 4g | Protein: 8g | Carbohydrates: 45g | Fiber: 4g

Ricotta and Berry Toast

Prep: 5 mins | Cook: 5 mins | Serves: 2

Ingredients:
- 4 slices whole grain bread
- 1 cup ricotta cheese
- 1 cup mixed berries (strawberries, blueberries, raspberries)
- 1 tablespoon honey or maple syrup
- Fresh mint for garnish

Instructions:
1. Toast the bread slices to your liking.
2. Spread a generous layer of ricotta cheese on each toast.
3. Top with mixed berries.
4. Drizzle with honey or maple syrup.
5. Garnish with fresh mint.
6. Serve immediately and enjoy!

Nutrition Facts: Calories: 320 | Fat: 12g | Protein: 15g | Carbohydrates: 40g | Fiber: 6g

Mediterranean Egg Salad on Whole Grain Bread

Prep: 10 mins | Cook: 10 mins | Serves: 4

Ingredients:
- 6 large eggs
- 2 tablespoons Greek yogurt
- 1 tablespoon mayonnaise
- 1 tablespoon Dijon mustard
- 1/4 cup red onion, finely chopped
- 1/4 cup celery, finely chopped
- 1/4 cup black olives, chopped
- Salt and pepper to taste
- 8 slices whole grain bread
- Fresh arugula or lettuce for serving

Instructions:
1. Place the eggs in a saucepan and cover with water. Bring to a boil, then reduce the heat and simmer for 9 minutes.
2. Transfer the eggs to a bowl of ice water and let them cool completely before peeling and chopping.
3. In a bowl, mix together the chopped eggs, Greek yogurt, mayonnaise, Dijon mustard, red onion, celery, and black olives. Season with salt and pepper to taste.
4. Spread the egg salad on 4 slices of bread, top with fresh arugula or lettuce, and cover with the remaining bread slices.
5. Cut in half and serve.

Nutrition Facts: Calories: 330 | Fat: 12g | Protein: 18g | Carbohydrates: 35g | Fiber: 6g

Pomegranate and Almond Oatmeal

Prep: 5 mins | Cook: 10 mins | Serves: 2

Ingredients:
- 1 cup old-fashioned oats
- 2 cups milk (dairy or plant-based)
- 1/4 teaspoon salt
- 1/2 cup pomegranate seeds
- 1/4 cup almonds, chopped
- 2 tablespoons honey or maple syrup
- A pinch of cinnamon (optional)

Instructions:
1. In a medium saucepan, bring the milk to a boil.
2. Add the oats and salt, reduce the heat to low, and cook, stirring occasionally, for 8-10 minutes, or until the oats are tender.
3. Remove from heat and stir in the pomegranate seeds, chopped almonds, and cinnamon if using.
4. Divide the oatmeal between two bowls, drizzle with honey or maple syrup, and serve.

Nutrition Facts: Calories: 320 | Fat: 10g | Protein: 12g | Carbohydrates: 50g | Fiber: 8g

Olive and Cheese Stuffed Omelette

Prep: 10 mins | Cook: 10 mins | Serves: 1

Ingredients:
- 3 large eggs
- 1/4 cup milk
- Salt and pepper to taste
- 1/4 cup green olives, chopped
- 1/4 cup feta cheese, crumbled
- 1 tablespoon olive oil
- Fresh herbs for garnish (optional)

Instructions:
1. In a bowl, whisk together the eggs, milk, salt, and pepper.
2. Heat the olive oil in a non-stick skillet over medium heat.
3. Pour in the egg mixture and let it cook undisturbed for 2-3 minutes, until the edges start to set.
4. Sprinkle the chopped olives and feta cheese over one half of the omelette.
5. Carefully fold the other half over the fillings and continue to cook for another 2-3 minutes, until the omelette is cooked through and the cheese is melted.
6. Slide the omelette onto a plate, garnish with fresh herbs if using, and serve.

Nutrition Facts: Calories: 350 | Fat: 25g | Protein: 20g | Carbohydrates: 8g | Fiber: 1g

Tomato and Basil Scrambled Tofu

Prep: 10 mins | Cook: 10 mins | Serves: 2

Ingredients:
- 1 block (14 oz) firm tofu, drained and crumbled
- 1 tablespoon olive oil
- 1 small onion, chopped
- 2 cloves garlic, minced
- 1 cup cherry tomatoes, halved
- A handful of fresh basil leaves, chopped
- Salt and pepper to taste
- Nutritional yeast for serving (optional)

Instructions:
1. Heat the olive oil in a skillet over medium heat. Add the onion and garlic, and sauté until the onion is translucent.
2. Add the crumbled tofu, tomatoes, basil, salt, and pepper. Cook, stirring occasionally, for 5-7 minutes, or until the tofu is heated through and the tomatoes are soft.
3. Taste and adjust the seasoning if necessary.
4. Divide the scramble between two plates, sprinkle with nutritional yeast if using, and serve.

Nutrition Facts: Calories: 220 | Fat: 13g | Protein: 18g | Carbohydrates: 10g | Fiber: 3g

Greek Yogurt with Honey and Pistachios

Prep: 5 mins | Serves: 1

Ingredients:
- 1 cup Greek yogurt
- 2 tablespoons honey
- 1/4 cup pistachios, chopped
- A pinch of ground cinnamon (optional)

Instructions:
1. Spoon the Greek yogurt into a bowl.
2. Drizzle with honey and sprinkle with chopped pistachios.
3. Add a pinch of ground cinnamon if using, and serve.

Nutrition Facts: Calories: 320 | Fat: 12g | Protein: 20g | Carbohydrates: 35g | Fiber: 2g

Mediterranean Vegan Breakfast Wrap

Prep: 15 mins | Cook: 10 mins | Serves: 2

Ingredients:
- 2 whole grain wraps
- 1 cup hummus
- 1 cup baby spinach leaves
- 1 cup roasted red pepper strips
- 1/2 cup Kalamata olives, pitted and halved
- 1/4 cup red onion, thinly sliced
- 1 tablespoon olive oil
- Salt and pepper to taste

Instructions:
1. Lay out the wraps on a flat surface and spread each with a layer of hummus.
2. Top with spinach leaves, roasted red pepper strips, Kalamata olives, and red onion.
3. Drizzle with olive oil, season with salt and pepper, and roll up tightly.
4. Optional: Heat a skillet over medium heat and grill the

wraps for 2-3 minutes on each side, or until crispy.
5. Cut in half and serve immediately.

Nutrition Facts: Calories: 400 | Fat: 20g | Protein: 12g | Carbohydrates: 45g | Fiber: 8g

Tomato and Feta Breakfast Casserole

Prep: 15 mins | Cook: 40 mins | Serves: 6

Ingredients:
• 8 large eggs
• 1 cup milk
• 2 cups cherry tomatoes, halved
• 1 cup feta cheese, crumbled
• 1/4 cup fresh basil, chopped
• 1/4 cup red onion, finely chopped
• 2 cloves garlic, minced
• Salt and pepper to taste
• 2 tablespoons olive oil

Instructions:
1. Preheat your oven to 350°F (175°C) and lightly grease a baking dish with olive oil.
2. In a large bowl, whisk together the eggs, milk, salt, and pepper.
3. Stir in the cherry tomatoes, feta cheese, basil, red onion, and garlic.
4. Pour the mixture into the prepared baking dish and bake for 35-40 minutes, or until the eggs are set and the top is golden brown.
5. Remove from oven and let it cool for a few minutes before serving.

Nutrition Facts: Calories: 220 | Fat: 16g | Protein: 13g | Carbohydrates: 8g | Fiber: 1g

Olive Oil and Dark Chocolate Granola

Prep: 10 mins | Cook: 30 mins | Serves: 8

Ingredients:
• 3 cups old-fashioned oats
• 1 cup nuts (almonds, walnuts, or a mix), chopped
• 1/2 cup honey or maple syrup
• 1/4 cup olive oil
• 1/2 teaspoon salt
• 1/2 cup dark chocolate chips
• 1 teaspoon vanilla extract

Instructions:
1. Preheat your oven to 300°F (150°C) and line a baking sheet with parchment paper.
2. In a large bowl, combine the oats, nuts, salt, and dark chocolate chips.
3. In a separate bowl, whisk together the honey or maple syrup, olive oil, and vanilla extract.
4. Pour the wet ingredients over the oat mixture and stir until everything is well coated.
5. Spread the granola out in an even layer on the prepared baking sheet.
6. Bake for 30 minutes, stirring every 10 minutes, until the granola is golden brown and crispy.
7. Let the granola cool completely before serving.

Nutrition Facts: Calories: 320 | Fat: 18g | Protein: 7g | Carbohydrates: 35g | Fiber: 5g

Mediterranean Breakfast Quinoa Salad

Prep: 10 mins | Cook: 15 mins | Serves: 4

Ingredients:
• 1 cup quinoa, rinsed
• 2 cups water or vegetable broth
• 1 cup cherry tomatoes, halved
• 1 cucumber, diced
• 1/4 cup red onion, finely chopped
• 1/4 cup Kalamata olives, pitted and chopped
• 1/4 cup feta cheese, crumbled
• 1/4 cup fresh parsley, chopped
• 2 tablespoons olive oil
• Juice of 1 lemon
• Salt and pepper to taste

Instructions:
1. In a medium saucepan, bring the water or vegetable broth to a boil.
2. Add the quinoa, reduce heat to low, cover, and simmer for 15 minutes, or until the quinoa is cooked and the liquid is absorbed.
3. Fluff the quinoa with a fork and transfer it to a large bowl.
4. Add the cherry tomatoes, cucumber, red onion, Kalamata olives, feta cheese, and parsley.
5. In a small bowl, whisk together the olive oil, lemon juice, salt, and pepper.
6. Pour the dressing over the quinoa salad and toss to combine.
7. Serve warm or at room temperature.

Nutrition Facts: Calories: 250 | Fat: 12g | Protein: 8g | Carbohydrates: 30g | Fiber: 4g

Baked Avocado Eggs with Pesto

Prep: 10 mins | Cook: 15 mins | Serves: 2

Ingredients:
• 1 ripe avocado, halved and pitted
• 2 large eggs
• 2 tablespoons pesto sauce
• Salt and pepper to taste
• Fresh basil for garnish

Instructions:
1. Preheat your oven to 400°F (200°C).
2. Place the avocado halves in a baking dish, cut side up. You may need to slice a small piece off the bottom to make them stable.
3. Carefully crack an egg into each avocado half. Season with salt and pepper.
4. Bake for 12-15 minutes, or until the eggs are cooked to your liking.
5. Drizzle with pesto sauce and garnish with fresh basil before serving.

Nutrition Facts: Calories: 300 | Fat: 25g | Protein: 10g | Carbohydrates: 10g | Fiber: 7g

Herb and Feta Stuffed Mushrooms

Prep: 15 mins | Cook: 20 mins | Serves: 4

Ingredients:
- 16 large button mushrooms, stems removed
- 1/2 cup feta cheese, crumbled
- 2 tablespoons fresh herbs (parsley, thyme, or basil), chopped
- 2 cloves garlic, minced
- 2 tablespoons olive oil
- Salt and pepper to taste

Instructions:
1. Preheat your oven to 375°F (190°C).
2. Place the mushroom caps on a baking sheet, stem side up.
3. In a small bowl, combine the feta cheese, fresh herbs, garlic, salt, and pepper.
4. Spoon the feta mixture into the mushroom caps and drizzle with olive oil.
5. Bake for 15-20 minutes, or until the mushrooms are tender and the filling is golden brown.
6. Serve warm.

Nutrition Facts: Calories: 120 | Fat: 9g | Protein: 6g | Carbohydrates: 5g | Fiber: 1g

Lemon Ricotta Pancakes

Prep: 10 mins | Cook: 15 mins | Serves: 4

Ingredients:
- 1 cup all-purpose flour
- 1 tablespoon sugar
- 2 teaspoons baking powder
- 1/2 teaspoon salt
- 1 cup ricotta cheese
- 3/4 cup milk
- 2 large eggs
- Zest and juice of 1 lemon
- 1 teaspoon vanilla extract
- Butter or oil for cooking
- Powdered sugar and fresh berries for serving

Instructions:
1. In a large bowl, whisk together the flour, sugar, baking powder, and salt.
2. In another bowl, combine the ricotta cheese, milk, eggs, lemon zest, lemon juice, and vanilla extract.
3. Add the wet ingredients to the dry ingredients and stir until just combined.
4. Heat a skillet or griddle over medium heat and add a small amount of butter or oil.
5. Pour 1/4 cup of batter onto the skillet for each pancake. Cook for 2-3 minutes or until bubbles form on the surface, then flip and cook for an additional 2-3 minutes or until golden brown and cooked through.
6. Serve warm with powdered sugar and fresh berries.

Nutrition Facts: Calories: 280 | Fat: 12g | Protein: 14g | Carbohydrates: 28g | Fiber: 1g

Greek Yogurt Smoothie Bowl with Fresh Fruit

Prep: 10 mins | Serves: 1

Ingredients:
- 1 cup Greek yogurt
- 1 banana, sliced
- 1/2 cup mixed berries (strawberries, blueberries, raspberries)
- 1 tablespoon honey or maple syrup
- A handful of granola
- Fresh fruit for topping (kiwi, mango, berries)
- A sprinkle of chia seeds or flaxseeds

Instructions:
1. In a blender, combine the Greek yogurt, banana, mixed berries, and honey or maple syrup. Blend until smooth.
2. Pour the smoothie into a bowl and top with granola, fresh fruit, and chia seeds or flaxseeds.
3. Serve immediately and enjoy your nutrient-packed breakfast.

Nutrition Facts: Calories: 320 | Fat: 5g | Protein: 15g | Carbohydrates: 55g | Fiber: 7g

Spiced Apple and Nut Porridge

Prep: 5 mins | Cook: 10 mins | Serves: 2

Ingredients:
- 1 cup oats
- 2 cups milk or water
- 1 apple, grated
- 1/2 teaspoon cinnamon
- 1/4 teaspoon nutmeg
- 1/4 cup chopped nuts (walnuts, almonds, or pecans)
- 1 tablespoon honey or maple syrup
- A pinch of salt

Instructions:
1. In a saucepan, combine the oats, milk or water, grated apple, cinnamon, nutmeg, and salt.
2. Bring to a boil, then reduce heat and simmer for 5-7 minutes, stirring occasionally, until the oats are cooked and the mixture has thickened.
3. Stir in the chopped nuts and sweeten with honey or maple syrup to taste.
4. Divide between two bowls and serve warm.

Nutrition Facts: Calories: 280 | Fat: 10g | Protein: 10g | Carbohydrates: 40g | Fiber: 6g

Mediterranean Veggie Breakfast Sandwich

Prep: 10 mins | Cook: 5 mins | Serves: 1

Ingredients:
- 1 whole grain English muffin, split and toasted
- 1 egg, cooked to your liking
- A handful of fresh spinach leaves
- 2 tomato slices
- 1/4 avocado, sliced

- 1 tablespoon hummus
- 1 tablespoon feta cheese, crumbled
- A pinch of salt and pepper

Instructions:
1. Spread hummus on the bottom half of the toasted English muffin.
2. Layer the fresh spinach, tomato slices, and avocado on top of the hummus.
3. Place the cooked egg on top of the vegetables, season with salt and pepper, and sprinkle with feta cheese.
4. Top with the other half of the English muffin and serve immediately.

Nutrition Facts: Calories: 350 | Fat: 16g | Protein: 15g | Carbohydrates: 36g | Fiber: 7g

Greek Oatmeal with Honey and Figs

Prep: 5 mins | Cook: 10 mins | Serves: 2

Ingredients:
- 1 cup oats
- 2 cups milk or water
- A pinch of salt
- 4-5 dried figs, chopped
- 1 tablespoon honey
- 1/2 teaspoon cinnamon
- 1/4 cup Greek yogurt
- Chopped nuts for topping (optional)

Instructions:
1. In a saucepan, bring the oats, milk or water, and salt to a boil.
2. Reduce heat and simmer for 5-7 minutes, stirring occasionally, until the oats are cooked and the mixture has thickened.
3. Stir in the chopped figs, honey, and cinnamon.
4. Divide the oatmeal between two bowls, top each with a dollop of Greek yogurt, and sprinkle with chopped nuts if using.
5. Serve warm and enjoy a taste of Greece in your breakfast bowl.

Nutrition Facts: Calories: 280 | Fat: 5g | Protein: 10g | Carbohydrates: 50g | Fiber: 7g

Tomato and Feta Baked Eggs

Prep: 5 mins | Cook: 15 mins | Serves: 2

Ingredients:
- 4 eggs
- 1 cup cherry tomatoes, halved
- 1/2 cup feta cheese, crumbled
- 1 tablespoon olive oil
- 1 clove garlic, minced
- Salt and pepper to taste
- Fresh basil leaves for garnish

Instructions:
1. Preheat your oven to 400°F (200°C).
2. In a skillet over medium heat, add the olive oil and garlic, sautéing until fragrant.
3. Add the cherry tomatoes and cook for 3-4 minutes until they start to soften.
4. Stir in half of the feta cheese and season with salt and pepper.
5. Make four wells in the tomato mixture and crack an egg into each well.
6. Sprinkle the remaining feta cheese over the top.
7. Transfer the skillet to the oven and bake for 8-10 minutes, or until the eggs are set to your liking.
8. Remove from oven, garnish with fresh basil, and serve immediately.

Nutrition Facts: Calories: 290 | Fat: 21g | Protein: 17g | Carbohydrates: 8g | Fiber: 2g

Mediterranean Breakfast Pita Pizza

Prep: 10 mins | Cook: 10 mins | Serves: 2

Ingredients:
- 2 whole wheat pita breads
- 1/4 cup hummus
- 1/2 cup cherry tomatoes, halved
- 1/4 red onion, thinly sliced
- 1/4 cup Kalamata olives, pitted and sliced
- 1/2 cup feta cheese, crumbled
- 1 tablespoon olive oil
- Salt and pepper to taste
- Fresh parsley for garnish

Instructions:
1. Preheat your oven to 400°F (200°C).
2. Place the pita breads on a baking sheet.
3. Spread hummus evenly over each pita.
4. Top with cherry tomatoes, red onion, olives, and feta cheese.
5. Drizzle with olive oil and season with salt and pepper.
6. Bake in the preheated oven for 8-10 minutes, or until the edges are crispy.
7. Remove from oven, garnish with fresh parsley, and cut into wedges before serving.

Nutrition Facts: Calories: 320 | Fat: 16g | Protein: 12g | Carbohydrates: 34g | Fiber: 6g

Hummus and Vegetable Breakfast Bowl

Prep: 10 mins | Serves: 1

Ingredients:
- 1 cup mixed greens (spinach, kale, arugula)
- 1/2 cup cherry tomatoes, halved
- 1/4 cucumber, sliced
- 1/4 cup hummus
- 1/4 avocado, sliced
- 1 boiled egg, peeled and halved
- 1 tablespoon olive oil
- Salt and pepper to taste
- Lemon wedge for serving

Instructions:
1. In a bowl, arrange the mixed greens as a base.
2. Top with cherry tomatoes, cucumber, hummus, avocado, and boiled egg.
3. Drizzle with olive oil and season with salt and pepper.

4. Serve with a lemon wedge on the side.

Nutrition Facts: Calories: 320 | Fat: 24g | Protein: 10g | Carbohydrates: 16g | Fiber: 7g

Greek Yogurt and Berry French Toast

Prep: 10 mins | Cook: 10 mins | Serves: 2

Ingredients:
• 4 slices whole grain bread
• 2 eggs
• 1/2 cup Greek yogurt
• 1/2 cup mixed berries (blueberries, strawberries, raspberries)
• 1 tablespoon honey or maple syrup
• 1 teaspoon vanilla extract
• Butter or oil for cooking
• Powdered sugar for serving

Instructions:
1. In a shallow dish, whisk together the eggs, Greek yogurt, and vanilla extract.
2. Heat a skillet over medium heat and add a small amount of butter or oil.
3. Dip each slice of bread into the egg mixture, ensuring both sides are well coated.
4. Place the coated bread slices in the skillet and cook for 3-4 minutes on each side or until golden brown and cooked through.
5. While the French toast is cooking, mix the berries with honey or maple syrup.
6. Serve the French toast warm, topped with the berry mixture and a sprinkle of powdered sugar.

Nutrition Facts: Calories: 350 | Fat: 12g | Protein: 14g | Carbohydrates: 46g | Fiber: 7g

Mediterranean Sweet Potato Hash

Prep: 10 mins | Cook: 20 mins | Serves: 2

Ingredients:
• 2 sweet potatoes, peeled and diced
• 1 bell pepper, diced
• 1 red onion, diced
• 2 cloves garlic, minced
• 1/4 cup feta cheese, crumbled
• 2 tablespoons olive oil
• Salt and pepper to taste
• 2 eggs (optional)
• Fresh parsley for garnish

Instructions:
1. Heat the olive oil in a large skillet over medium heat.
2. Add the sweet potatoes, bell pepper, and red onion. Cook for 15-20 minutes, stirring occasionally, until the vegetables are tender and caramelized.
3. Stir in the garlic and cook for an additional minute until fragrant.
4. Season with salt and pepper, and stir in the feta cheese.
5. If using, make two wells in the hash and crack an egg into each well. Cover the skillet and cook for 3-4 minutes or until the eggs are set to your liking.
6. Garnish with fresh parsley and serve immediately.

Nutrition Facts: Calories: 350 | Fat: 15g | Protein: 10g | Carbohydrates: 45g | Fiber: 8g

Lemon and Blueberry Quinoa Pancakes

Prep: 15 mins | Cook: 15 mins | Serves: 4

Ingredients:
• 1 cup cooked quinoa
• 1 cup all-purpose flour
• 2 teaspoons baking powder
• 1/4 cup sugar
• Zest of 1 lemon
• 1 cup milk (any kind)
• 2 large eggs
• 1 teaspoon vanilla extract
• 1 cup fresh blueberries
• Butter or oil for cooking

Instructions:
1. In a large bowl, combine the cooked quinoa, flour, baking powder, sugar, and lemon zest.
2. In another bowl, whisk together the milk, eggs, and vanilla extract.
3. Add the wet ingredients to the dry ingredients, stirring just until combined.
4. Fold in the blueberries.
5. Heat a skillet over medium heat and add a small amount of butter or oil.
6. Pour 1/4 cup of batter onto the skillet for each pancake, cooking for 2-3 minutes on each side or until golden brown and cooked through.
7. Serve warm with additional blueberries and syrup if desired.

Nutrition Facts: Calories: 220 | Fat: 4g | Protein: 8g | Carbohydrates: 38g | Fiber: 3g

Greek Breakfast Wrap with Spinach and Feta

Prep: 10 mins | Cook: 5 mins | Serves: 2

Ingredients:
• 2 whole wheat wraps
• 2 cups fresh spinach leaves
• 1/2 cup feta cheese, crumbled
• 1 tomato, sliced
• 1/4 red onion, thinly sliced
• 2 tablespoons hummus
• 1 tablespoon olive oil
• Salt and pepper to taste

Instructions:
1. In a skillet, heat the olive oil over medium heat.
2. Add the spinach and sauté until wilted, about 2-3 minutes. Season with salt and pepper.
3. Lay out the wraps and spread 1 tablespoon of hummus on each.
4. Divide the sautéed spinach, feta cheese, tomato slices, and red onion between the wraps.
5. Fold in the sides and roll up tightly.
6. Serve immediately or wrap in parchment for a on-the-

go breakfast.

Nutrition Facts: Calories: 310 | Fat: 14g | Protein: 12g | Carbohydrates: 36g | Fiber: 5g

Mediterranean Avocado and Egg Breakfast Bowl

Prep: 10 mins | Cook: 5 mins | Serves: 1

Ingredients:
• 1 egg
• 1/2 avocado, sliced
• 1/2 cup cherry tomatoes, halved
• 1/4 cup cucumber, diced
• 1/4 cup red onion, thinly sliced
• 1 tablespoon olive oil
• 1 tablespoon feta cheese, crumbled
• Salt and pepper to taste
• Fresh herbs for garnish (such as parsley or dill)

Instructions:
1. In a skillet, cook the egg to your preference (fried, scrambled, or poached).
2. In a bowl, arrange the avocado slices, cherry tomatoes, cucumber, and red onion.
3. Top with the cooked egg and sprinkle with feta cheese.
4. Drizzle with olive oil and season with salt and pepper.
5. Garnish with fresh herbs and serve immediately.

Nutrition Facts: Calories: 330 | Fat: 25g | Protein: 11g | Carbohydrates: 16g | Fiber: 7g

Olive and Tomato Frittata Muffins

Prep: 10 mins | Cook: 20 mins | Serves: 6

Ingredients:
• 6 eggs
• 1/2 cup milk
• 1/2 cup cherry tomatoes, quartered
• 1/4 cup Kalamata olives, pitted and chopped
• 1/4 cup feta cheese, crumbled
• 1 tablespoon olive oil
• Salt and pepper to taste
• Fresh basil for garnish

Instructions:
1. Preheat your oven to 350°F (175°C) and grease a muffin tin.
2. In a bowl, whisk together the eggs, milk, salt, and pepper.
3. Stir in the cherry tomatoes, olives, and feta cheese.
4. Pour the mixture into the muffin tin, filling each cup 3/4 of the way full.
5. Bake for 18-20 minutes or until the eggs are set.
6. Remove from oven, let cool for 5 minutes before removing from the tin.
7. Garnish with fresh basil and serve warm.

Nutrition Facts: Calories: 120 | Fat: 9g | Protein: 7g | Carbohydrates: 3g | Fiber: 0g

Greek Yogurt with Fresh Peaches and Honey

Prep: 5 mins | Serves: 1

Ingredients:
• 1 cup Greek yogurt
• 1 fresh peach, sliced
• 1 tablespoon honey
• 1 tablespoon almonds, chopped

Instructions:
1. In a bowl, layer the Greek yogurt and peach slices.
2. Drizzle with honey and sprinkle with chopped almonds.
3. Serve immediately and enjoy a refreshing breakfast.

Nutrition Facts: Calories: 210 | Fat: 6g | Protein: 15g | Carbohydrates: 25g | Fiber: 2g

Chapter 4: Lunch

Greek Salad with Grilled Chicken

Prep: 15 mins | Cook: 10 mins | Serves: 4

Ingredients:
- 2 boneless, skinless chicken breasts
- 1 tablespoon olive oil
- Salt and pepper to taste
- 6 cups mixed salad greens
- 1 cup cherry tomatoes, halved
- 1 cucumber, sliced
- 1/2 red onion, thinly sliced
- 1/2 cup Kalamata olives, pitted
- 1/2 cup feta cheese, crumbled
- For the dressing:
- 3 tablespoons olive oil
- 1 tablespoon red wine vinegar
- 1 teaspoon Dijon mustard
- 1 garlic clove, minced
- Salt and pepper to taste

Instructions:
1. Preheat grill to medium-high heat.
2. Rub chicken breasts with olive oil and season with salt and pepper.
3. Grill chicken for 5-6 minutes per side or until fully cooked.
4. Remove from grill and let rest for 5 minutes before slicing.
5. In a large bowl, combine salad greens, cherry tomatoes, cucumber, red onion, Kalamata olives, and feta cheese.
6. In a small bowl, whisk together the dressing ingredients.
7. Add the grilled chicken to the salad and drizzle with dressing.
8. Toss everything together and serve immediately.

Nutrition Facts: Calories: 320 | Fat: 18g | Protein: 25g | Carbohydrates: 12g | Fiber: 3g

Quinoa Tabbouleh with Fresh Herbs

Prep: 15 mins | Cook: 15 mins | Serves: 4

Ingredients:
- 1 cup quinoa
- 2 cups water
- 1 cup fresh parsley, chopped
- 1/2 cup fresh mint, chopped
- 3 tomatoes, diced
- 1 cucumber, diced
- 1/4 red onion, finely chopped
- 3 tablespoons olive oil
- Juice of 1 lemon
- Salt and pepper to taste

Instructions:
1. In a medium saucepan, bring water to a boil.
2. Add quinoa, reduce heat to low, cover, and cook for 15 minutes or until quinoa is cooked.
3. Remove from heat and let cool.
4. In a large bowl, combine cooked quinoa, parsley, mint, tomatoes, cucumber, and red onion.

5. In a small bowl, whisk together olive oil, lemon juice, salt, and pepper.
6. Pour dressing over quinoa mixture and toss to combine.
7. Serve chilled or at room temperature.

Nutrition Facts: Calories: 220 | Fat: 10g | Protein: 6g | Carbohydrates: 30g | Fiber: 5g

Lemon Basil Pesto Pasta Salad

Prep: 10 mins | Cook: 10 mins | Serves: 4

Ingredients:
- 8 oz whole wheat pasta
- 1 cup fresh basil leaves
- 1/4 cup Parmesan cheese, grated
- 2 tablespoons pine nuts
- 2 garlic cloves
- Zest and juice of 1 lemon
- 1/4 cup olive oil
- Salt and pepper to taste
- 1 cup cherry tomatoes, halved
- 1/4 red onion, thinly sliced

Instructions:
1. Cook pasta according to package directions. Drain and let cool.
2. In a food processor, combine basil, Parmesan, pine nuts, garlic, lemon zest, and lemon juice.
3. With the processor running, slowly add the olive oil until smooth.
4. Season pesto with salt and pepper.
5. In a large bowl, combine cooked pasta, cherry tomatoes, red onion, and pesto.
6. Toss until everything is well coated.
7. Serve chilled or at room temperature.

Nutrition Facts: Calories: 350 | Fat: 18g | Protein: 10g | Carbohydrates: 38g | Fiber: 6g

Mediterranean Chickpea and Feta Wraps

Prep: 10 mins | Serves: 4

Ingredients:
- 4 whole wheat wraps
- 1 can (15 oz) chickpeas, drained and rinsed
- 1/2 cup feta cheese, crumbled
- 1 cup mixed salad greens
- 1 tomato, sliced
- 1/2 cucumber, sliced
- 1/4 red onion, thinly sliced
- 2 tablespoons hummus
- 2 tablespoons Greek yogurt
- Salt and pepper to taste

Instructions:
1. Lay out the wraps on a flat surface.
2. Spread each wrap with hummus.
3. Divide chickpeas, feta cheese, salad greens, tomato, cucumber, and red onion between the wraps.
4. In a small bowl, mix Greek yogurt with a pinch of salt and pepper. Drizzle over the fillings.

5. Fold in the sides of the wraps and roll up tightly.
6. Cut in half and serve immediately.

Nutrition Facts: Calories: 310 | Fat: 9g | Protein: 14g | Carbohydrates: 46g | Fiber: 8g

Grilled Eggplant and Hummus Sandwich

Prep: 10 mins | Cook: 10 mins | Serves: 4

Ingredients:
- 1 large eggplant, sliced into 1/2 inch rounds
- 2 tablespoons olive oil
- Salt and pepper to taste
- 8 slices whole grain bread
- 1 cup hummus
- 2 tomatoes, sliced
- 1/4 red onion, thinly sliced
- 2 cups arugula or spinach

Instructions:
1. Preheat grill to medium-high heat.
2. Brush eggplant slices with olive oil and season with salt and pepper.
3. Grill eggplant for 4-5 minutes per side or until tender and grill marks appear.
4. To assemble the sandwiches, spread 2 tablespoons of hummus on each slice of bread.
5. Layer grilled eggplant, tomato slices, red onion, and arugula on 4 slices of bread.
6. Top with remaining slices of bread, hummus side down.
7. Cut in half and serve immediately.

Nutrition Facts: Calories: 330 | Fat: 15g | Protein: 11g | Carbohydrates: 38g | Fiber: 9g

Spinach and Feta Stuffed Portobello Mushrooms

Prep: 15 mins | Cook: 15 mins | Serves: 4

Ingredients:
- 4 large portobello mushrooms, stems removed
- 2 tablespoons olive oil
- 3 cloves garlic, minced
- 5 cups fresh spinach
- 1/2 cup crumbled feta cheese
- 1/4 cup breadcrumbs
- 1/4 cup grated Parmesan cheese
- Salt and pepper to taste
- Fresh basil for garnish

Instructions:
1. Preheat your oven to 375°F (190°C) and line a baking sheet with parchment paper.
2. Place the portobello mushrooms on the baking sheet, gill side up.
3. In a large skillet over medium heat, add the olive oil and garlic. Sauté until fragrant.
4. Add the spinach and cook until wilted. Season with salt and pepper.
5. In a bowl, combine the cooked spinach, feta cheese,

breadcrumbs, and Parmesan cheese.
6. Fill each mushroom cap with the spinach and cheese mixture, pressing down to compact.
7. Bake in the preheated oven for 15 minutes, or until the mushrooms are tender and the tops are golden.
8. Garnish with fresh basil before serving.

Nutrition Facts: Calories: 200 | Fat: 12g | Protein: 10g | Carbohydrates: 15g | Fiber: 4g

Roasted Red Pepper and Lentil Soup

Prep: 10 mins | Cook: 30 mins | Serves: 4

Ingredients:
- 2 tablespoons olive oil
- 1 onion, diced
- 3 cloves garlic, minced
- 1 carrot, diced
- 1 stalk celery, diced
- 1 jar (12 oz) roasted red peppers, drained and chopped
- 1 cup dry red lentils
- 4 cups vegetable broth
- 1 teaspoon ground cumin
- 1/2 teaspoon paprika
- Salt and pepper to taste
- Fresh cilantro for garnish

Instructions:
1. In a large pot over medium heat, add the olive oil, onion, garlic, carrot, and celery. Sauté until the vegetables are softened.
2. Add the roasted red peppers, red lentils, vegetable broth, cumin, and paprika. Bring to a boil.
3. Reduce the heat and simmer for 25-30 minutes, or until the lentils are tender.
4. Use an immersion blender to puree the soup until smooth, or transfer to a blender in batches.
5. Season with salt and pepper to taste.
6. Serve hot, garnished with fresh cilantro.

Nutrition Facts: Calories: 250 | Fat: 5g | Protein: 14g | Carbohydrates: 40g | Fiber: 18g

Tuna, Olive and Caper Salad

Prep: 10 mins | Serves: 4

Ingredients:
- 2 cans (5 oz each) tuna in olive oil, drained
- 1/2 cup Kalamata olives, pitted and halved
- 1/4 cup capers, drained
- 1/4 red onion, finely chopped
- 1 cup cherry tomatoes, halved
- 1/4 cup fresh parsley, chopped
- Juice of 1 lemon
- 3 tablespoons olive oil
- Salt and pepper to taste
- Mixed salad greens for serving

Instructions:
1. In a large bowl, combine the tuna, olives, capers, red onion, cherry tomatoes, and parsley.
2. In a small bowl, whisk together the lemon juice, olive oil, salt, and pepper.

3. Pour the dressing over the tuna mixture and toss to combine.
4. Serve the salad over a bed of mixed salad greens.

Nutrition Facts: Calories: 280 | Fat: 16g | Protein: 20g | Carbohydrates: 10g | Fiber: 3g

Mediterranean Falafel Bowl

Prep: 15 mins | Cook: 5 mins | Serves: 4

Ingredients:
• 2 cups cooked falafel (store-bought or homemade)
• 2 cups cooked quinoa or brown rice
• 1 cup cherry tomatoes, halved
• 1 cucumber, diced
• 1/2 red onion, thinly sliced
• 1/2 cup Kalamata olives, pitted and halved
• 1/2 cup hummus
• 1/4 cup tzatziki sauce
• Fresh parsley for garnish

Instructions:
1. If using store-bought falafel, follow the package instructions to heat.
2. In each of four bowls, place 1/2 cup of quinoa or brown rice.
3. Top each bowl with falafel, cherry tomatoes, cucumber, red onion, and olives.
4. Add a dollop of hummus and a drizzle of tzatziki to each bowl.
5. Garnish with fresh parsley before serving.

Nutrition Facts: Calories: 450 | Fat: 15g | Protein: 15g | Carbohydrates: 65g | Fiber: 10g

Greek-Style Stuffed Bell Peppers

Prep: 20 mins | Cook: 30 mins | Serves: 4

Ingredients:
• 4 bell peppers, halved and seeds removed
• 2 tablespoons olive oil
• 1 onion, diced
• 3 cloves garlic, minced
• 1 pound ground turkey or chicken
• 1 can (14 oz) diced tomatoes, drained
• 1 cup cooked brown rice
• 1/2 cup crumbled feta cheese
• 1/2 cup chopped Kalamata olives
• 1 teaspoon dried oregano
• Salt and pepper to taste
• Fresh parsley for garnish

Instructions:
1. Preheat your oven to 375°F (190°C).
2. Place the bell pepper halves cut-side up in a baking dish.
3. In a large skillet over medium heat, add the olive oil, onion, and garlic. Sauté until the onion is translucent.
4. Add the ground turkey or chicken and cook until browned.
5. Stir in the diced tomatoes, brown rice, feta cheese, olives, oregano, salt, and pepper.
6. Spoon the mixture into the bell pepper halves.
7. Cover the baking dish with foil and bake for 25

minutes.
8. Remove the foil and bake for an additional 5 minutes, or until the peppers are tender.
9. Garnish with fresh parsley before serving.

Nutrition Facts: Calories: 350 | Fat: 15g | Protein: 25g | Carbohydrates: 30g | Fiber: 6g

Tomato, Cucumber, and Avocado Salad

Prep: 10 mins | Serves: 4

Ingredients:
• 2 large ripe tomatoes, diced
• 1 English cucumber, diced
• 2 avocados, diced
• 1/4 red onion, thinly sliced
• 1/4 cup fresh cilantro, chopped
• Juice of 2 limes
• 3 tablespoons olive oil
• Salt and pepper to taste

Instructions:
1. In a large bowl, combine the tomatoes, cucumber, avocados, red onion, and cilantro.
2. In a small bowl, whisk together the lime juice, olive oil, salt, and pepper.
3. Pour the dressing over the salad and gently toss to combine.
4. Serve immediately, or refrigerate for up to an hour before serving.

Nutrition Facts: Calories: 220 | Fat: 16g | Protein: 3g | Carbohydrates: 18g | Fiber: 7g

Lemon Garlic Shrimp and Asparagus

Prep: 10 mins | Cook: 10 mins | Serves: 4

Ingredients:
• 1 pound shrimp, peeled and deveined
• 1 bunch asparagus, trimmed and cut into 2-inch pieces
• 3 tablespoons olive oil
• 4 cloves garlic, minced
• Zest and juice of 1 lemon
• Salt and pepper to taste
• Fresh parsley for garnish

Instructions:
1. In a large skillet over medium-high heat, add 2 tablespoons of olive oil.
2. Add the shrimp to the skillet and cook for 2-3 minutes per side, or until pink and cooked through.
3. Remove the shrimp from the skillet and set aside.
4. In the same skillet, add the remaining 1 tablespoon of olive oil and the asparagus. Cook for 3-4 minutes, or until tender-crisp.
5. Add the garlic, lemon zest, and lemon juice to the skillet and cook for an additional 1 minute.
6. Return the shrimp to the skillet and toss to combine. Season with salt and pepper.
7. Serve hot, garnished with fresh parsley.

Nutrition Facts: Calories: 200 | Fat: 12g | Protein: 20g | Carbohydrates: 6g | Fiber: 2g

Spiced Lamb Pita Pockets

Prep: 15 mins | Cook: 15 mins | Serves: 4

Ingredients:
- 1 pound ground lamb
- 1 tablespoon olive oil
- 1 onion, diced
- 3 cloves garlic, minced
- 1 teaspoon ground cumin
- 1 teaspoon ground coriander
- 1/2 teaspoon ground cinnamon
- Salt and pepper to taste
- 4 pita breads
- 1 cup Greek yogurt
- 1 cucumber, diced
- 1 tomato, diced
- Fresh mint for garnish

Instructions:
1. In a large skillet over medium-high heat, add the olive oil and lamb. Cook until browned, breaking up with a spatula.
2. Add the onion and garlic to the skillet and cook for an additional 5 minutes, or until the onion is translucent.
3. Stir in the cumin, coriander, cinnamon, salt, and pepper. Cook for an additional 2 minutes.
4. Warm the pita breads in the oven or on a skillet.
5. To assemble the pita pockets, spread a layer of Greek yogurt inside each pita, then fill with the lamb mixture, cucumber, and tomato.
6. Garnish with fresh mint before serving.

Nutrition Facts: Calories: 550 | Fat: 32g | Protein: 30g | Carbohydrates: 35g | Fiber: 4g

Mediterranean Cauliflower Rice Salad

Prep: 15 mins | Cook: 5 mins | Serves: 4

Ingredients:
- 4 cups cauliflower rice
- 1 cup cherry tomatoes, halved
- 1 cucumber, diced
- 1/2 red onion, finely chopped
- 1/2 cup Kalamata olives, halved
- 1/2 cup feta cheese, crumbled
- 1/4 cup fresh parsley, chopped
- 3 tablespoons olive oil
- Juice of 1 lemon
- Salt and pepper to taste

Instructions:
1. In a large skillet over medium heat, add the cauliflower rice and cook for 5 minutes, or until tender.
2. Remove from heat and let cool.
3. In a large bowl, combine the cooked cauliflower rice, cherry tomatoes, cucumber, red onion, olives, feta cheese, and parsley.
4. In a small bowl, whisk together the olive oil, lemon juice, salt, and pepper.
5. Pour the dressing over the salad and toss to combine.

6. Serve chilled or at room temperature.

Nutrition Facts: Calories: 220 | Fat: 15g | Protein: 7g | Carbohydrates: 15g | Fiber: 5g

Grilled Vegetable and Quinoa Salad

Prep: 15 mins | Cook: 15 mins | Serves: 4

Ingredients:
- 1 zucchini, sliced into rounds
- 1 red bell pepper, sliced
- 1 yellow bell pepper, sliced
- 1 red onion, sliced into rings
- 2 tablespoons olive oil
- Salt and pepper to taste
- 2 cups cooked quinoa
- 1/4 cup fresh basil, chopped
- 3 tablespoons balsamic vinegar
- 1/4 cup feta cheese, crumbled

Instructions:
1. Preheat grill to medium-high heat.
2. Toss the zucchini, bell peppers, and red onion with olive oil, salt, and pepper.
3. Grill the vegetables for 3-4 minutes per side, or until charred and tender.
4. In a large bowl, combine the grilled vegetables, quinoa, and fresh basil.
5. Drizzle with balsamic vinegar and toss to combine.
6. Serve warm or at room temperature, topped with crumbled feta cheese.

Nutrition Facts: Calories: 250 | Fat: 10g | Protein: 8g | Carbohydrates: 35g | Fiber: 5g

Mediterranean Turkey and Hummus Sandwich

Prep: 5 mins | Serves: 1

Ingredients:
- 2 slices whole grain bread
- 3 ounces sliced turkey breast
- 2 tablespoons hummus
- 1/4 cup mixed greens
- 2 slices tomato
- 2 slices cucumber
- 1 tablespoon feta cheese, crumbled
- 1 teaspoon olive oil
- Salt and pepper to taste

Instructions:
1. Lay out the slices of bread on a clean surface.
2. Spread the hummus evenly over one side of each slice of bread.
3. On one slice of bread, layer the turkey, mixed greens, tomato, and cucumber.
4. Sprinkle the feta cheese over the vegetables, and drizzle with olive oil. Season with salt and pepper to taste.
5. Place the other slice of bread on top, hummus side down.
6. Press down gently, and cut the sandwich in half. Serve immediately.

Nutrition Facts: Calories: 350 | Fat: 12g | Protein: 25g | Carbohydrates: 35g | Fiber: 5g

Greek Lentil Salad with Feta

Prep: 10 mins | Serves: 4

Ingredients:
• 2 cups cooked lentils
• 1 cup cherry tomatoes, halved
• 1 cucumber, diced
• 1/2 red onion, finely chopped
• 1/2 cup Kalamata olives, halved
• 1/2 cup feta cheese, crumbled
• 3 tablespoons olive oil
• Juice of 1 lemon
• 1 teaspoon dried oregano
• Salt and pepper to taste
• Fresh parsley for garnish

Instructions:
1. In a large bowl, combine the lentils, cherry tomatoes, cucumber, red onion, olives, and feta cheese.
2. In a small bowl, whisk together the olive oil, lemon juice, oregano, salt, and pepper.
3. Pour the dressing over the salad and toss to combine.
4. Garnish with fresh parsley before serving. Serve chilled or at room temperature.

Nutrition Facts: Calories: 250 | Fat: 14g | Protein: 12g | Carbohydrates: 24g | Fiber: 8g

Mediterranean Grilled Cheese with Olive Tapenade

Prep: 5 mins | Cook: 5 mins | Serves: 1

Ingredients:
• 2 slices whole grain bread
• 1/4 cup shredded mozzarella cheese
• 1 tablespoon olive tapenade
• 2 slices tomato
• Handful of spinach leaves
• 1 tablespoon butter

Instructions:
1. Lay out the slices of bread on a clean surface.
2. Spread the olive tapenade on one side of each slice of bread.
3. On one slice of bread, layer the mozzarella cheese, tomato slices, and spinach leaves.
4. Top with the other slice of bread, tapenade side down.
5. In a skillet over medium heat, melt the butter.
6. Place the sandwich in the skillet, and cook for 2-3 minutes on each side, or until the bread is golden brown and the cheese is melted.
7. Remove from the skillet, cut in half, and serve immediately.

Nutrition Facts: Calories: 400 | Fat: 20g | Protein: 15g | Carbohydrates: 40g | Fiber: 5g

Lemon Herb Chicken Salad

Prep: 15 mins | Cook: 10 mins | Serves: 4

Ingredients:
• 2 boneless, skinless chicken breasts
• Juice and zest of 1 lemon
• 2 tablespoons olive oil
• 1 teaspoon dried oregano
• 1 teaspoon dried basil
• Salt and pepper to taste
• 6 cups mixed greens
• 1 cup cherry tomatoes, halved
• 1/4 red onion, thinly sliced
• 1/4 cup feta cheese, crumbled
• Balsamic vinaigrette for dressing

Instructions:
1. Preheat grill or skillet over medium-high heat.
2. In a bowl, combine the lemon juice, zest, olive oil, oregano, basil, salt, and pepper.
3. Add the chicken breasts to the marinade, ensuring they are well coated. Let sit for 5 minutes.
4. Grill the chicken for 5-7 minutes on each side or until fully cooked.
5. Slice the grilled chicken into strips.
6. In a large salad bowl, toss the mixed greens, cherry tomatoes, red onion, and grilled chicken.
7. Sprinkle with feta cheese, and drizzle with balsamic vinaigrette.
8. Serve immediately.

Nutrition Facts: Calories: 250 | Fat: 12g | Protein: 25g | Carbohydrates: 10g | Fiber: 3g

Mediterranean Vegan Buddha Bowl

Prep: 15 mins | Serves: 1

Ingredients:
• 1 cup cooked quinoa
• 1/2 cup chickpeas, drained and rinsed
• 1/2 cup cucumber, diced
• 1/2 cup cherry tomatoes, halved
• 1/4 cup red bell pepper, diced
• 1/4 cup red cabbage, shredded
• 1/4 cup hummus
• 1 tablespoon olive oil
• Juice of 1 lemon
• Salt and pepper to taste
• Fresh parsley for garnish

Instructions:
1. In a large bowl, arrange the quinoa, chickpeas, cucumber, cherry tomatoes, red bell pepper, and red cabbage.
2. Place a dollop of hummus in the center of the bowl.
3. Drizzle the olive oil and lemon juice over the bowl. Season with salt and pepper.
4. Garnish with fresh parsley before serving.
5. Mix everything together before eating, and enjoy!

Nutrition Facts: Calories: 450 | Fat: 14g | Protein: 15g | Carbohydrates: 65g | Fiber: 10g

Greek Zucchini Noodles with Feta and Olives

Prep: 15 mins | Cook: 5 mins | Serves: 2

Ingredients:
• 2 large zucchinis, spiralized into noodles
• 1/2 cup cherry tomatoes, halved
• 1/4 cup Kalamata olives, pitted and sliced
• 1/4 cup red onion, thinly sliced
• 1/4 cup feta cheese, crumbled
• 2 tablespoons olive oil
• Juice of 1 lemon
• 1 teaspoon dried oregano
• Salt and pepper to taste
• Fresh parsley for garnish

Instructions:
1. In a large skillet over medium heat, add the olive oil.
2. Add the zucchini noodles and sauté for 2-3 minutes until just tender.
3. Remove from heat and transfer to a large bowl.
4. Add the cherry tomatoes, olives, red onion, feta cheese, lemon juice, dried oregano, salt, and pepper.
5. Toss everything together until well combined.
6. Garnish with fresh parsley and serve immediately.

Nutrition Facts: Calories: 200 | Fat: 15g | Protein: 5g | Carbohydrates: 10g | Fiber: 3g

Chickpea and Roasted Vegetable Salad

Prep: 10 mins | Cook: 20 mins | Serves: 4

Ingredients:
• 1 can chickpeas, drained and rinsed
• 2 cups mixed vegetables (bell peppers, zucchini, cherry tomatoes), chopped
• 3 tablespoons olive oil, divided
• Salt and pepper to taste
• 1/4 cup red onion, thinly sliced
• 1/4 cup feta cheese, crumbled
• Juice of 1 lemon
• 1 teaspoon dried basil
• Fresh parsley for garnish

Instructions:
1. Preheat the oven to 400°F (200°C).
2. Place the mixed vegetables on a baking sheet, drizzle with 2 tablespoons of olive oil, and season with salt and pepper.
3. Roast in the oven for 20 minutes, or until the vegetables are tender and slightly charred.
4. In a large bowl, combine the roasted vegetables, chickpeas, red onion, and feta cheese.
5. In a small bowl, whisk together the remaining 1 tablespoon of olive oil, lemon juice, and dried basil.
6. Pour the dressing over the salad and toss to combine.
7. Garnish with fresh parsley before serving. Serve warm or at room temperature.

Nutrition Facts: Calories: 250 | Fat: 12g | Protein: 8g | Carbohydrates: 30g | Fiber: 8g

Mediterranean Stuffed Avocado

Prep: 10 mins | Serves: 2

Ingredients:
• 2 ripe avocados, halved and pitted
• 1 cup canned tuna, drained
• 1/4 cup cherry tomatoes, halved
• 1/4 cup cucumber, diced
• 1/4 cup red onion, finely chopped
• 2 tablespoons Kalamata olives, pitted and sliced
• Juice of 1 lemon
• 2 tablespoons olive oil
• Salt and pepper to taste
• Fresh parsley for garnish

Instructions:
1. Scoop out some of the avocado flesh to create a larger cavity for the filling, dice the scooped-out flesh.
2. In a bowl, mix together the tuna, cherry tomatoes, cucumber, red onion, Kalamata olives, diced avocado, lemon juice, olive oil, salt, and pepper.
3. Spoon the tuna mixture back into the avocado halves.
4. Garnish with fresh parsley and serve immediately.

Nutrition Facts: Calories: 320 | Fat: 26g | Protein: 15g | Carbohydrates: 14g | Fiber: 7g

Lemon and Artichoke Pasta

Prep: 10 mins | Cook: 15 mins | Serves: 4

Ingredients:
• 8 oz whole wheat pasta
• 1 can artichoke hearts, drained and quartered
• 2 tablespoons olive oil
• 3 garlic cloves, minced
• Zest and juice of 1 lemon
• Salt and pepper to taste
• 1/4 cup Parmesan cheese, grated
• Fresh basil for garnish

Instructions:
1. Cook the pasta according to package instructions until al dente. Drain and set aside.
2. In a large skillet over medium heat, heat the olive oil.
3. Add the garlic and sauté for 1 minute, or until fragrant.
4. Add the artichoke hearts, lemon zest, lemon juice, salt, and pepper. Sauté for 5 minutes, or until the artichokes are heated through.
5. Add the cooked pasta and toss to combine.
6. Sprinkle with Parmesan cheese and toss again.
7. Garnish with fresh basil and serve immediately.

Nutrition Facts: Calories: 320 | Fat: 10g | Protein: 12g | Carbohydrates: 46g | Fiber: 8g

Greek Chicken Gyro Salad

Prep: 15 mins | Cook: 15 mins | Serves: 4

Ingredients:
- 1 lb chicken breast, thinly sliced
- 1 tablespoon olive oil
- 1 teaspoon dried oregano
- Salt and pepper to taste
- 6 cups mixed greens
- 1 cup cherry tomatoes, halved
- 1 cucumber, diced
- 1/4 red onion, thinly sliced
- 1/4 cup Kalamata olives, pitted and sliced
- 1/4 cup feta cheese, crumbled
- Tzatziki sauce for dressing

Instructions:
1. In a skillet over medium-high heat, add the olive oil.
2. Add the chicken, oregano, salt, and pepper. Cook for 6-8 minutes, or until the chicken is cooked through.
3. In a large salad bowl, combine the mixed greens, cherry tomatoes, cucumber, red onion, olives, and feta cheese.
4. Add the cooked chicken to the salad.
5. Drizzle with tzatziki sauce before serving.

Nutrition Facts: Calories: 300 | Fat: 12g | Protein: 30g | Carbohydrates: 18g | Fiber: 4g

Mediterranean Bean and Barley Salad

Prep: 15 mins | Cook: 40 mins | Serves: 4

Ingredients:
- 1 cup pearled barley
- 1 can (15 oz) white beans, drained and rinsed
- 1 cucumber, diced
- 1 bell pepper, diced
- 1/4 cup red onion, finely chopped
- 1/4 cup Kalamata olives, pitted and sliced
- 1/4 cup feta cheese, crumbled
- 1/4 cup fresh parsley, chopped
- 3 tablespoons olive oil
- Juice of 1 lemon
- Salt and pepper to taste

Instructions:
1. In a medium saucepan, bring 3 cups of water to a boil. Add the barley, reduce heat, and simmer covered for 30-40 minutes, or until tender. Drain any excess water and let it cool.
2. In a large bowl, combine the cooled barley, white beans, cucumber, bell pepper, red onion, olives, and feta cheese.
3. In a small bowl, whisk together the olive oil, lemon juice, salt, and pepper.
4. Pour the dressing over the salad and toss to combine.
5. Stir in the fresh parsley and serve. This salad can be served immediately or refrigerated for later use.

Nutrition Facts: Calories: 340 | Fat: 11g | Protein: 12g | Carbohydrates: 51g | Fiber: 12g

Roasted Eggplant and Pita Sandwich

Prep: 10 mins | Cook: 20 mins | Serves: 4

Ingredients:
- 1 large eggplant, sliced into rounds
- 2 tablespoons olive oil
- Salt and pepper to taste
- 4 pita bread rounds
- 1/4 cup hummus
- 1 cucumber, thinly sliced
- 1 tomato, thinly sliced
- 1/4 red onion, thinly sliced
- Fresh parsley for garnish

Instructions:
1. Preheat your oven to 425°F (220°C) and line a baking sheet with parchment paper.
2. Place the eggplant slices on the baking sheet, brush both sides with olive oil, and season with salt and pepper.
3. Roast in the oven for 20 minutes, flipping halfway through, until the eggplant is tender and golden brown.
4. To assemble the sandwiches, spread hummus on each pita bread.
5. Top with roasted eggplant slices, cucumber, tomato, and red onion.
6. Garnish with fresh parsley and fold the pita over the filling. Serve immediately.

Nutrition Facts: Calories: 290 | Fat: 9g | Protein: 8g | Carbohydrates: 45g | Fiber: 7g

Lemon and Dill Salmon Salad

Prep: 15 mins | Cook: 15 mins | Serves: 4

Ingredients:
- 4 salmon fillets
- 2 tablespoons olive oil
- Salt and pepper to taste
- Juice and zest of 1 lemon
- 1 tablespoon fresh dill, chopped
- 6 cups mixed greens
- 1 cucumber, sliced
- 1/4 red onion, thinly sliced
- 1/4 cup feta cheese, crumbled

Instructions:
1. Preheat your grill or grill pan over medium-high heat.
2. Brush the salmon fillets with olive oil, season with salt and pepper, and grill for 6-7 minutes per side, or until fully cooked.
3. In a small bowl, combine the lemon juice, lemon zest, and fresh dill.
4. In a large salad bowl, toss together the mixed greens, cucumber, red onion, and feta cheese.
5. Top the salad with the grilled salmon fillets.
6. Drizzle the lemon and dill mixture over the top and serve immediately.

Nutrition Facts: Calories: 320 | Fat: 18g | Protein: 28g | Carbohydrates: 10g | Fiber: 3g

Mediterranean Pesto and Mozzarella Panini

Prep: 10 mins | Cook: 5 mins | Serves: 4

Ingredients:
- 8 slices whole grain bread
- 1/4 cup pesto sauce
- 8 slices fresh mozzarella cheese
- 1 tomato, sliced
- 1/4 red onion, thinly sliced
- 1/4 cup fresh basil leaves
- 2 tablespoons olive oil

Instructions:
1. Spread a tablespoon of pesto on 4 slices of bread.
2. Top each with 2 slices of mozzarella, tomato slices, red onion, and fresh basil.
3. Top with the remaining slices of bread.
4. Brush the outside of each sandwich with olive oil.
5. Heat a panini press or grill pan over medium-high heat.
6. Grill the sandwiches for 2-3 minutes on each side, until the bread is toasted and the cheese has melted.
7. Slice in half and serve immediately.

Nutrition Facts: Calories: 420 | Fat: 26g | Protein: 18g | Carbohydrates: 30g | Fiber: 4g

Grilled Halloumi and Vegetable Skewers

Prep: 20 mins | Cook: 10 mins | Serves: 4

Ingredients:
- 8 oz halloumi cheese, cut into cubes
- 1 zucchini, cut into chunks
- 1 bell pepper, cut into chunks
- 1 red onion, cut into chunks
- 2 tablespoons olive oil
- Salt and pepper to taste
- Juice of 1 lemon
- Fresh parsley for garnish

Instructions:
1. Preheat your grill or grill pan to medium-high heat.
2. Thread the halloumi, zucchini, bell pepper, and red onion onto skewers.
3. Brush the skewers with olive oil and season with salt and pepper.
4. Grill for 10-12 minutes, turning occasionally, until the vegetables are tender and the cheese is golden brown.
5. Drizzle with lemon juice and garnish with fresh parsley before serving

Nutrition Facts: Calories: 320 | Fat: 22g | Protein: 16g | Carbohydrates: 16g | Fiber: 3g

Greek Quinoa and Avocado Salad

Prep: 15 mins | Cook: 15 mins | Serves: 4

Ingredients:
- 1 cup quinoa, rinsed
- 2 cups water
- 1 avocado, diced
- 1 cucumber, diced
- 1 cup cherry tomatoes, halved
- 1/4 cup red onion, finely chopped
- 1/4 cup Kalamata olives, pitted and chopped
- 1/4 cup feta cheese, crumbled
- Juice of 1 lemon
- 3 tablespoons olive oil
- 1 tablespoon fresh oregano, chopped
- Salt and pepper to taste

Instructions:
1. In a medium saucepan, bring the water to a boil. Add the quinoa, reduce heat, cover, and simmer for 15 minutes or until quinoa is cooked. Fluff with a fork and let cool.
2. In a large bowl, combine the cooled quinoa, avocado, cucumber, cherry tomatoes, red onion, olives, and feta cheese.
3. In a small bowl, whisk together the lemon juice, olive oil, oregano, salt, and pepper.
4. Pour the dressing over the salad and toss to combine.
5. Serve immediately or chill in the refrigerator for later.

Nutrition Facts: Calories: 310 | Fat: 18g | Protein: 8g | Carbohydrates: 30g | Fiber: 6g

Mediterranean Tuna and White Bean Salad

Prep: 10 mins | Serves: 4

Ingredients:
- 2 cans (15 oz each) white beans, drained and rinsed
- 1 can (5 oz) tuna in olive oil, drained
- 1/4 cup red onion, finely chopped
- 1/4 cup fresh parsley, chopped
- 2 tablespoons capers, drained
- Juice of 1 lemon
- 3 tablespoons olive oil
- Salt and pepper to taste

Instructions:
1. In a large bowl, combine the white beans, tuna, red onion, parsley, and capers.
2. In a small bowl, whisk together the lemon juice, olive oil, salt, and pepper.
3. Pour the dressing over the salad and toss to combine.
4. Serve immediately, or chill in the refrigerator for later.

Nutrition Facts: Calories: 330 | Fat: 10g | Protein: 23g | Carbohydrates: 37g | Fiber: 10g

Chickpea and Spinach Stew

Prep: 10 mins | Cook: 30 mins | Serves: 4

Ingredients:
- 1 tablespoon olive oil
- 1 onion, diced
- 3 cloves garlic, minced
- 1 can (15 oz) chickpeas, drained and rinsed
- 1 can (14.5 oz) diced tomatoes
- 2 teaspoons ground cumin
- 1 teaspoon paprika
- 1/2 teaspoon cayenne pepper
- 4 cups fresh spinach
- Salt and pepper to taste
- Juice of 1 lemon

Instructions:
1. Heat the olive oil in a large pot over medium heat. Add the onion and garlic and sauté until the onion is translucent.
2. Stir in the chickpeas, diced tomatoes, cumin, paprika, and cayenne pepper. Bring to a simmer and cook for 20 minutes.
3. Add the spinach and cook until wilted. Season with salt, pepper, and lemon juice.
4. Serve hot, either alone or over rice or quinoa.

Nutrition Facts: Calories: 220 | Fat: 4g | Protein: 11g | Carbohydrates: 37g | Fiber: 9g

Greek Lemon and Rice Soup

Prep: 10 mins | Cook: 30 mins | Serves: 4

Ingredients:
- 6 cups chicken or vegetable broth
- 1/2 cup long-grain white rice
- 3 eggs
- Juice of 3 lemons
- 1 teaspoon salt
- 1/2 teaspoon black pepper
- Fresh parsley for garnish

Instructions:
1. In a large pot, bring the broth to a boil. Add the rice, reduce heat, and simmer for 20 minutes or until rice is cooked.
2. In a separate bowl, beat the eggs and lemon juice together.
3. Slowly ladle a cup of the hot broth into the egg mixture, whisking constantly to prevent the eggs from curdling.
4. Stir the egg mixture back into the pot. Season with salt and pepper.
5. Cook on low heat for an additional 5 minutes, stirring constantly, until the soup has thickened slightly.
6. Serve hot, garnished with fresh parsley.

Nutrition Facts: Calories: 200 | Fat: 5g | Protein: 10g | Carbohydrates: 30g | Fiber: 1g

Mediterranean Caprese Salad

Prep: 10 mins | Serves: 4

Ingredients:
- 4 ripe tomatoes, sliced
- 1/4 pound fresh mozzarella cheese, sliced
- 1/4 cup fresh basil leaves
- 1/4 cup extra-virgin olive oil
- Balsamic glaze for drizzling
- Salt and pepper to taste

Instructions:
1. Arrange the tomato and mozzarella slices on a platter, overlapping and alternating them.
2. Tuck whole basil leaves in between the slices.
3. Drizzle with olive oil and balsamic glaze.
4. Season with salt and pepper.
5. Serve immediately as a refreshing appetizer or side dish.

Nutrition Facts: Calories: 250 | Fat: 20g | Protein: 12g | Carbohydrates: 8g | Fiber: 2g

Eggplant, Tomato, and Chickpea Casserole

Prep: 15 mins | Cook: 35 mins | Serves: 4

Ingredients:
- 1 large eggplant, cut into 1/2-inch slices
- 2 tablespoons olive oil
- 1 can (15 oz) chickpeas, drained and rinsed
- 1 can (14.5 oz) diced tomatoes
- 1 onion, diced
- 3 cloves garlic, minced
- 1 teaspoon ground cumin
- 1/2 teaspoon ground coriander
- 1/4 teaspoon cayenne pepper
- Salt and pepper to taste
- Fresh parsley for garnish

Instructions:
1. Preheat your oven to 375°F (190°C).
2. Place the eggplant slices on a baking sheet, brush with olive oil, and season with salt and pepper. Roast for 20 minutes or until tender.
3. In a large skillet over medium heat, sauté the onion and garlic in the remaining olive oil until the onion is translucent.
4. Add the chickpeas, diced tomatoes, cumin, coriander, and cayenne pepper. Stir well and cook for another 5 minutes.
5. In a casserole dish, layer the roasted eggplant slices and chickpea mixture. Bake for 15 minutes.
6. Garnish with fresh parsley before serving.

Nutrition Facts: Calories: 220 | Fat: 8g | Protein: 7g | Carbohydrates: 31g | Fiber: 9g

Mediterranean Chicken and Orzo Salad

Prep: 15 mins | Cook: 15 mins | Serves: 4

Ingredients:
- 1 cup orzo pasta
- 2 cups cooked chicken, shredded
- 1 cucumber, diced
- 1 cup cherry tomatoes, halved
- 1/4 cup red onion, finely chopped
- 1/4 cup Kalamata olives, pitted and chopped
- 1/4 cup feta cheese, crumbled
- 3 tablespoons olive oil
- Juice of 1 lemon
- 1 tablespoon fresh oregano, chopped, Salt and pepper to taste

Instructions:
1. Cook the orzo according to the package instructions, then drain and rinse under cold water.
2. In a large bowl, combine the cooked orzo, shredded chicken, cucumber, cherry tomatoes, red onion, olives, and feta cheese.
3. In a small bowl, whisk together the olive oil, lemon juice, oregano, salt, and pepper.
4. Pour the dressing over the salad and toss to combine.
5. Serve chilled or at room temperature.

Nutrition Facts: Calories: 350 | Fat: 15g | Protein: 22g | Carbohydrates: 30g | Fiber: 3g

Spiced Moroccan Lentil Soup

Prep: 10 mins | Cook: 40 mins | Serves: 4

Ingredients:
- 1 cup dried lentils, rinsed and drained
- 1 onion, diced
- 3 cloves garlic, minced
- 2 carrots, peeled and diced
- 2 teaspoons ground cumin
- 1 teaspoon ground coriander
- 1/2 teaspoon ground cinnamon
- 1/2 teaspoon cayenne pepper
- 4 cups vegetable broth
- 1 can (14.5 oz) diced tomatoes
- Salt and pepper to taste
- Fresh cilantro for garnish

Instructions:
1. In a large pot, sauté the onion, garlic, and carrots in olive oil until the onion is translucent.
2. Add the cumin, coriander, cinnamon, and cayenne pepper, stirring well to combine.
3. Add the lentils, vegetable broth, and diced tomatoes. Bring to a boil, then reduce heat and simmer for 30 minutes or until lentils are tender.
4. Season with salt and pepper to taste.
5. Serve hot, garnished with fresh cilantro.

Nutrition Facts: Calories: 230 | Fat: 2g | Protein: 13g | Carbohydrates: 42g | Fiber: 15g

Grilled Zucchini and Feta Salad

Prep: 10 mins | Cook: 10 mins | Serves: 4

Ingredients:
- 2 large zucchini, sliced lengthwise
- 2 tablespoons olive oil
- Salt and pepper to taste
- 1 cup mixed salad greens
- 1/2 cup feta cheese, crumbled
- 2 tablespoons balsamic vinegar
- Fresh mint leaves for garnish

Instructions:
1. Preheat a grill or grill pan over medium-high heat.
2. Brush the zucchini slices with olive oil and season with salt and pepper.
3. Grill the zucchini for 3-4 minutes on each side, or until tender and grill marks appear.
4. Arrange the grilled zucchini on a platter over a bed of salad greens.
5. Sprinkle with feta cheese and drizzle with balsamic vinegar.
6. Garnish with fresh mint leaves and serve immediately.

Nutrition Facts: Calories: 160 | Fat: 11g | Protein: 5g | Carbohydrates: 11g | Fiber: 2g

Mediterranean Turkey and Quinoa Salad

Prep: 15 mins | Cook: 15 mins | Serves: 4

Ingredients:
- 1 cup quinoa, rinsed
- 2 cups water
- 2 cups cooked turkey, chopped
- 1 cucumber, diced
- 1 cup cherry tomatoes, halved
- 1/4 cup red onion, finely chopped
- 1/4 cup Kalamata olives, pitted and chopped
- 1/4 cup feta cheese, crumbled
- 3 tablespoons olive oil
- Juice of 1 lemon
- 1 tablespoon fresh oregano, chopped
- Salt and pepper to taste

Instructions:
1. In a medium saucepan, bring the water to a boil. Add the quinoa, reduce heat, cover, and simmer for 15 minutes or until quinoa is cooked. Fluff with a fork and let cool.
2. In a large bowl, combine the cooled quinoa, chopped turkey, cucumber, cherry tomatoes, red onion, olives, and feta cheese.
3. In a small bowl, whisk together the olive oil, lemon juice, oregano, salt, and pepper.
4. Pour the dressing over the salad and toss to combine.
5. Serve immediately or chill in the refrigerator for later.

Nutrition Facts: Calories: 330 | Fat: 15g | Protein: 22g | Carbohydrates: 30g | Fiber: 5g

Roasted Red Pepper Hummus Wrap

Prep: 10 mins | Serves: 2

Ingredients:
- 2 whole grain tortillas
- 1 cup roasted red pepper hummus
- 1 cup fresh spinach leaves
- 1/2 cucumber, thinly sliced
- 1/2 bell pepper, thinly sliced
- 1/4 red onion, thinly sliced
- 1/4 cup feta cheese, crumbled

Instructions:
1. Lay out the tortillas on a flat surface.
2. Spread each tortilla with 1/2 cup of roasted red pepper hummus.
3. Divide the spinach leaves between the two wraps.
4. Layer the cucumber slices, bell pepper slices, and red onion slices over the spinach.
5. Sprinkle each wrap with 2 tablespoons of feta cheese.
6. Fold in the sides of the tortilla and roll up tightly.
7. Slice in half and serve immediately.

Nutrition Facts: Calories: 350 | Fat: 15g | Protein: 12g | Carbohydrates: 45g | Fiber: 8g

Greek-Style Farro Salad

Prep: 10 mins | Cook: 30 mins | Serves: 4

Ingredients:
- 1 cup farro, rinsed
- 2 cups cherry tomatoes, halved
- 1 cucumber, diced
- 1/2 red onion, finely chopped
- 1/2 cup Kalamata olives, pitted and halved
- 1/2 cup feta cheese, crumbled
- 1/4 cup fresh parsley, chopped
- 3 tablespoons olive oil
- Juice of 1 lemon
- Salt and pepper to taste

Instructions:
1. Cook the farro according to package instructions, then drain and let cool.
2. In a large bowl, combine the cooled farro, cherry tomatoes, cucumber, red onion, olives, feta cheese, and parsley.
3. In a small bowl, whisk together the olive oil, lemon juice, salt, and pepper.
4. Pour the dressing over the salad and toss to combine.
5. Serve immediately or chill in the refrigerator for later.

Nutrition Facts: Calories: 340 | Fat: 15g | Protein: 10g | Carbohydrates: 45g | Fiber: 8g

Mediterranean Salmon and Quinoa Bowl

Prep: 15 mins | Cook: 15 mins | Serves: 4

Ingredients:
- 4 salmon fillets
- 1 cup quinoa, rinsed
- 2 cups water
- 1 cup cherry tomatoes, halved
- 1 cucumber, diced
- 1/2 red onion, thinly sliced
- 1/4 cup Kalamata olives, pitted and halved
- 1/4 cup feta cheese, crumbled
- 3 tablespoons olive oil, Juice of 1 lemon
- Salt and pepper to taste, Fresh parsley for garnish

Instructions:
1. Cook the quinoa in 2 cups of water according to package instructions, then fluff with a fork and let cool.
2. Season the salmon fillets with salt and pepper.
3. Heat 1 tablespoon of olive oil in a skillet over medium-high heat.
4. Add the salmon fillets and cook for 3-4 minutes on each side or until cooked through.
5. In a large bowl, combine the cooled quinoa, cherry tomatoes, cucumber, red onion, olives, and feta cheese.
6. Drizzle with the remaining 2 tablespoons of olive oil and the lemon juice. Toss to combine.
7. Divide the quinoa salad between four bowls.
8. Top each bowl with a cooked salmon fillet.
9. Garnish with fresh parsley and serve immediately.

Nutrition Facts: Calories: 420 | Fat: 20g | Protein: 30g | Carbohydrates: 30g | Fiber: 5g

Spinach, Olive, and Feta Tart

Prep: 15 mins | Cook: 25 mins | Serves: 6

Ingredients:
- 1 sheet puff pastry, thawed
- 2 cups fresh spinach leaves
- 1/2 cup Kalamata olives, pitted and chopped
- 1/2 cup feta cheese, crumbled
- 2 eggs
- 1/4 cup milk
- Salt and pepper to taste

Instructions:
1. Preheat your oven to 375°F (190°C).
2. Roll out the puff pastry on a floured surface and transfer to a tart pan, trimming any excess pastry.
3. In a bowl, whisk together the eggs, milk, salt, and pepper.
4. Spread the spinach leaves over the pastry.
5. Sprinkle with the chopped olives and crumbled feta cheese.
6. Pour the egg mixture over the top.
7. Bake for 25 minutes or until the tart is golden brown and set.
8. Let cool for a few minutes before slicing and serving.

Nutrition Facts: Calories: 320 | Fat: 22g | Protein: 8g | Carbohydrates: 20g | Fiber: 2g

Mediterranean Shrimp and Couscous

Prep: 10 mins | Cook: 10 mins | Serves: 4

Ingredients:
• 1 cup couscous
• 1 pound shrimp, peeled and deveined
• 2 tablespoons olive oil
• 1 cup cherry tomatoes, halved
• 1 cucumber, diced
• 1/4 cup feta cheese, crumbled
• 1/4 cup fresh parsley, chopped
• Juice of 1 lemon
• Salt and pepper to taste

Instructions:
1. Cook the couscous according to package instructions, then fluff with a fork and let cool.
2. Heat the olive oil in a skillet over medium-high heat.
3. Add the shrimp, salt, and pepper, and cook for 2-3 minutes on each side or until cooked through.
4. In a large bowl, combine the cooked couscous, cooked shrimp, cherry tomatoes, cucumber, feta cheese, and parsley.
5. Drizzle with the lemon juice and toss to combine.
6. Serve immediately or chill in the refrigerator for later.

Nutrition Facts: Calories: 340 | Fat: 10g | Protein: 25g | Carbohydrates: 35g | Fiber: 3g

Greek Yogurt and Cucumber Soup

Prep: 10 mins | Serves: 4

Ingredients:
• 2 large cucumbers, peeled and diced
• 2 cups Greek yogurt
• 2 cloves garlic, minced
• Juice of 1 lemon
• 2 tablespoons fresh dill, chopped
• Salt and pepper to taste
• 1 tablespoon olive oil
• Fresh dill for garnish

Instructions:
1. In a blender or food processor, combine the cucumbers, Greek yogurt, minced garlic, lemon juice, and chopped dill.
2. Blend until smooth.
3. Season with salt and pepper to taste.
4. Chill in the refrigerator for at least 30 minutes before serving.
5. Drizzle with olive oil and garnish with fresh dill before serving.

Nutrition Facts: Calories: 120 | Fat: 4g | Protein: 8g | Carbohydrates: 12g | Fiber: 1g

Mediterranean Vegetable and Chickpea Salad

Prep: 15 mins | Serves: 4

Ingredients:
• 1 can (15 oz) chickpeas, drained and rinsed
• 1 cucumber, diced
• 1 bell pepper, diced
• 1 pint cherry tomatoes, halved
• 1/4 red onion, finely chopped
• 1/4 cup Kalamata olives, pitted and halved
• 1/4 cup feta cheese, crumbled
• 3 tablespoons olive oil
• Juice of 1 lemon
• 2 tablespoons fresh parsley, chopped
• Salt and pepper to taste

Instructions:
1. In a large bowl, combine the chickpeas, cucumber, bell pepper, cherry tomatoes, red onion, olives, and feta cheese.
2. In a small bowl, whisk together the olive oil, lemon juice, parsley, salt, and pepper.
3. Pour the dressing over the salad and toss to combine.
4. Serve immediately or chill in the refrigerator for later.

Nutrition Facts: Calories: 250 | Fat: 13g | Protein: 9g | Carbohydrates: 29g | Fiber: 7g

Grilled Chicken and Tzatziki Salad

Prep: 20 mins | Cook: 10 mins | Serves: 4

Ingredients:
• 4 boneless, skinless chicken breasts
• 2 tablespoons olive oil
• Salt and pepper to taste
• 6 cups mixed salad greens
• 1 cucumber, sliced
• 1 cup cherry tomatoes, halved
• 1/2 red onion, thinly sliced
• 1/2 cup tzatziki sauce
• Fresh dill for garnish

Instructions:
1. Preheat grill to medium-high heat.
2. Brush the chicken breasts with olive oil and season with salt and pepper.
3. Grill for 5-7 minutes on each side or until cooked through.
4. Let the chicken rest for 5 minutes before slicing.
5. In a large bowl, combine the salad greens, cucumber slices, cherry tomatoes, and red onion slices.
6. Top the salad with the grilled chicken slices and drizzle with tzatziki sauce.
7. Garnish with fresh dill and serve immediately.

Nutrition Facts: Calories: 280 | Fat: 11g | Protein: 30g | Carbohydrates: 14g | Fiber: 3g

Tomato, Olive, and Basil Focaccia Sandwich

Prep: 10 mins | Serves: 4

Ingredients:
- 1 loaf focaccia bread, cut into 4 pieces
- 1/4 cup olive tapenade
- 2 tomatoes, sliced
- 1/4 red onion, thinly sliced
- 8 fresh basil leaves
- 1/4 cup feta cheese, crumbled
- 2 tablespoons balsamic vinegar

Instructions:
1. Spread each piece of focaccia with olive tapenade.
2. Layer with tomato slices, red onion slices, and basil leaves.
3. Sprinkle with feta cheese.
4. Drizzle with balsamic vinegar.
5. Serve immediately or wrap in parchment paper for on-the-go.

Nutrition Facts: Calories: 300 | Fat: 11g | Protein: 9g | Carbohydrates: 41g | Fiber: 3g

Roasted Cauliflower and Quinoa Salad with Lemon Tahini Dressing

Prep: 10 mins | Cook: 20 mins | Serves: 4

Ingredients:
- 1 head cauliflower, cut into florets
- 2 tablespoons olive oil
- Salt and pepper to taste
- 1 cup quinoa, rinsed
- 2 cups water
- 1/4 cup tahini
- Juice of 1 lemon
- 2 tablespoons water
- 2 tablespoons fresh parsley, chopped
- 1/4 cup pomegranate seeds

Instructions:
1. Preheat oven to 425°F (220°C).
2. Toss the cauliflower florets with olive oil, salt, and pepper.
3. Spread in a single layer on a baking sheet and roast for 20 minutes, or until golden and tender.
4. While the cauliflower is roasting, combine the quinoa and water in a medium saucepan.
5. Bring to a boil, then reduce heat and simmer, covered, for 15 minutes, or until quinoa is cooked.
6. In a small bowl, whisk together the tahini, lemon juice, and water until smooth.
7. Fluff the cooked quinoa with a fork and transfer to a large bowl.
8. Add the roasted cauliflower, fresh parsley, and pomegranate seeds.
9. Drizzle with the lemon tahini dressing and toss to combine.
10. Serve warm or at room temperature.

Nutrition Facts: Calories: 310 | Fat: 14g | Protein: 10g | Carbohydrates: 38g | Fiber: 7g

Chapter 5: Dinner

Grilled Mediterranean Chicken Kebabs

Prep: 25 mins | Cook: 10 mins | Serves: 4

Ingredients:
- 1 lb boneless, skinless chicken breasts, cut into 1-inch cubes
- 2 bell peppers, cut into 1-inch pieces
- 1 red onion, cut into 1-inch pieces
- 1 zucchini, cut into 1-inch slices
- 1/4 cup olive oil
- Juice of 1 lemon
- 3 cloves garlic, minced
- 1 tsp dried oregano
- Salt and pepper to taste
- Wooden skewers, soaked in water for 30 minutes

Instructions:
1. Preheat grill to medium-high heat.
2. Thread chicken, bell peppers, red onion, and zucchini onto the soaked skewers, alternating between each.
3. In a small bowl, whisk together olive oil, lemon juice, minced garlic, dried oregano, salt, and pepper.
4. Brush the kebabs with the olive oil mixture.
5. Grill for 10-12 minutes, turning occasionally, until chicken is cooked through and vegetables are tender, serve immediately.

Nutrition Facts: Calories: 275 | Fat: 12g | Protein: 28g | Carbohydrates: 12g | Fiber: 2g

Baked Cod with Olives and Capers

Prep: 10 mins | Cook: 20 mins | Serves: 4

Ingredients:
- 4 cod fillets
- 2 tbsp olive oil
- 1/2 cup Kalamata olives, pitted and halved
- 2 tbsp capers, drained
- 1 pint cherry tomatoes, halved
- Juice of 1 lemon
- Salt and pepper to taste
- Fresh parsley for garnish

Instructions:
1. Preheat oven to 400°F (200°C).
2. Place the cod fillets in a baking dish.
3. Drizzle with olive oil and sprinkle with salt and pepper.
4. Scatter the olives, capers, and cherry tomatoes around the fish.
5. Squeeze the lemon juice over the top.
6. Bake for 20 minutes, or until fish flakes easily with a fork.
7. Garnish with fresh parsley before serving.

Nutrition Facts: Calories: 220 | Fat: 8g | Protein: 30g | Carbohydrates: 8g | Fiber: 2g

Greek Lemon Roasted Potatoes

Prep: 10 mins | Cook: 40 mins | Serves: 4

Ingredients:
- 6 medium potatoes, peeled and quartered
- 1/4 cup olive oil
- Juice of 2 lemons
- 3 cloves garlic, minced
- 1 tsp dried oregano
- Salt and pepper to taste
- Fresh parsley for garnish

Instructions:
1. Preheat oven to 400°F (200°C).
2. Place the potatoes in a baking dish.
3. In a bowl, mix together the olive oil, lemon juice, minced garlic, dried oregano, salt, and pepper.
4. Pour the mixture over the potatoes, tossing to coat.
5. Bake for 40 minutes, or until potatoes are golden and crispy.
6. Garnish with fresh parsley before serving.

Nutrition Facts: Calories: 280 | Fat: 7g | Protein: 6g | Carbohydrates: 50g | Fiber: 5g

Mediterranean Stuffed Bell Peppers

Prep: 15 mins | Cook: 30 mins | Serves: 4

Ingredients:
- 4 bell peppers, halved and seeds removed
- 1 cup cooked quinoa
- 1 can (15 oz) black beans, drained and rinsed
- 1 cup cherry tomatoes, halved
- 1/4 cup red onion, finely chopped
- 1/4 cup feta cheese, crumbled
- 2 tbsp olive oil
- Juice of 1 lemon
- 2 cloves garlic, minced
- Salt and pepper to taste
- Fresh parsley for garnish

Instructions:
1. Preheat oven to 375°F (190°C).
2. Place the bell pepper halves in a baking dish, cut side up.
3. In a bowl, mix together the cooked quinoa, black beans, cherry tomatoes, red onion, and feta cheese.
4. Fill each bell pepper half with the quinoa mixture.
5. In another bowl, whisk together the olive oil, lemon juice, minced garlic, salt, and pepper.
6. Drizzle the olive oil mixture over the stuffed bell peppers.
7. Bake for 30 minutes, or until peppers are tender.
8. Garnish with fresh parsley before serving.

Nutrition Facts: Calories: 250 | Fat: 10g | Protein: 9g | Carbohydrates: 33g | Fiber: 9g

Spaghetti with Garlic and Olive Oil

Prep: 5 mins | Cook: 10 mins | Serves: 4

Ingredients:
- 12 oz spaghetti
- 1/4 cup olive oil
- 4 cloves garlic, thinly sliced
- 1/4 tsp red pepper flakes (optional)
- Salt to taste
- Fresh parsley, chopped for garnish
- Grated Parmesan cheese for serving

Instructions:
1. Cook the spaghetti according to package directions until al dente. Drain and set aside.
2. In a large skillet over medium heat, add the olive oil.
3. Add the garlic slices and red pepper flakes if using. Sauté until garlic is golden brown.
4. Add the cooked spaghetti to the skillet, tossing to coat in the garlic oil.
5. Season with salt to taste.
6. Serve garnished with chopped parsley and grated Parmesan cheese.

Nutrition Facts: Calories: 380 | Fat: 14g | Protein: 10g | Carbohydrates: 56g | Fiber: 3g

Lemon and Oregano Grilled Shrimp

Prep: 15 mins | Cook: 8 mins | Serves: 4

Ingredients:
- 1 lb large shrimp, peeled and deveined
- 3 tbsp olive oil
- Zest and juice of 1 lemon
- 3 cloves garlic, minced
- 1 tbsp fresh oregano, chopped
- Salt and pepper to taste
- Lemon wedges for serving

Instructions:
1. In a bowl, combine the olive oil, lemon zest, lemon juice, garlic, oregano, salt, and pepper.
2. Add the shrimp and toss to coat. Marinate in the refrigerator for at least 30 minutes.
3. Preheat the grill to medium-high heat.
4. Thread the shrimp onto skewers and grill for 3-4 minutes per side, until opaque and cooked through.
5. Serve with lemon wedges on the side.

Nutrition Facts: Calories: 200 | Fat: 10g | Protein: 24g | Carbohydrates: 3g | Fiber: 0g

Greek Moussaka with Bechamel Sauce

Prep: 30 mins | Cook: 1 hr | Serves: 6

Ingredients:
- 2 large eggplants, sliced
- Olive oil
- 1 lb ground lamb or beef
- 1 large onion, chopped
- 3 cloves garlic, minced
- 1 can (14 oz) crushed tomatoes
- 1/4 cup red wine
- 1 tsp cinnamon
- 1 tsp allspice
- Salt and pepper to taste
- 1/4 cup all-purpose flour
- 1/4 cup butter
- 2 cups milk
- Nutmeg to taste
- 1/2 cup Parmesan cheese, grated

Instructions:
1. Preheat the oven to 400°F (200°C).
2. Brush the eggplant slices with olive oil and season with salt. Place them on a baking sheet in a single layer.
3. Bake for 20 minutes, or until softened. Reduce oven temperature to 350°F (175°C).
4. In a skillet, heat some olive oil over medium heat. Add the ground meat, breaking it up with a spoon, and cook until browned.
5. Add the onion and garlic, and cook for an additional 5 minutes.
6. Stir in the crushed tomatoes, red wine, cinnamon, allspice, salt, and pepper. Simmer for 15 minutes.
7. In a saucepan, melt the butter over medium heat. Stir in the flour and cook for 2 minutes.
8. Gradually whisk in the milk until smooth. Continue to cook, stirring constantly, until the sauce thickens.
9. Season with salt, pepper, and nutmeg. Remove from heat and stir in the Parmesan cheese.
10. In a baking dish, layer the eggplant slices and meat sauce. Repeat the layers, finishing with a layer of eggplant.
11. Pour the bechamel sauce over the top, spreading it out evenly.
12. Bake for 30 minutes, or until golden and bubbly.
13. Allow to cool for 10 minutes before slicing and serving.

Nutrition Facts: Calories: 420 | Fat: 27g | Protein: 21g | Carbohydrates: 24g | Fiber: 6g

Mediterranean Lamb Chops with Rosemary

Prep: 15 mins | Cook: 10 mins | Serves: 4

Ingredients:
- 8 lamb chops
- 1/4 cup olive oil
- Juice of 1 lemon
- 4 cloves garlic, minced
- 2 tbsp fresh rosemary, chopped
- Salt and pepper to taste

Instructions:
1. In a bowl, whisk together the olive oil, lemon juice, garlic, rosemary, salt, and pepper.
2. Add the lamb chops, turning to coat. Marinate in the refrigerator for at least 2 hours.
3. Preheat the grill to medium-high heat.
4. Grill the lamb chops for 4-5 minutes per side, or until they reach your desired level of doneness.
5. Let rest for 5 minutes before serving.

Nutrition Facts: Calories: 370 | Fat: 28g | Protein: 24g | Carbohydrates: 1g | Fiber: 0g

Baked Feta with Tomatoes and Olives

Prep: 10 mins | Cook: 20 mins | Serves: 4

Ingredients:
- 200g feta cheese
- 1 cup cherry tomatoes, halved
- 1/2 cup Kalamata olives, pitted
- 3 tbsp olive oil
- 2 cloves garlic, minced
- 1 tsp dried oregano
- Fresh basil for garnish
- Crusty bread for serving

Instructions:
1. Preheat the oven to 400°F (200°C).
2. Place the feta cheese in the center of a baking dish.
3. Surround with the cherry tomatoes and olives.
4. Drizzle with olive oil and sprinkle with garlic and oregano.
5. Bake for 20 minutes, or until the feta is soft and the tomatoes are roasted.
6. Garnish with fresh basil and serve with crusty bread.

Nutrition Facts: Calories: 280 | Fat: 23g | Protein: 10g | Carbohydrates: 9g | Fiber: 2g

Grilled Swordfish with Lemon and Herbs

Prep: 15 mins | Cook: 10 mins | Serves: 4

Ingredients:
- 4 swordfish steaks
- 3 tablespoons olive oil
- Juice of 2 lemons
- 3 garlic cloves, minced
- 2 tablespoons fresh parsley, chopped
- 1 tablespoon fresh rosemary, chopped
- 1 tablespoon fresh oregano, chopped
- Salt and pepper to taste
- Lemon wedges for serving

Instructions:
1. Preheat grill to medium-high heat.
2. In a bowl, combine olive oil, lemon juice, garlic, parsley, rosemary, oregano, salt, and pepper.
3. Brush both sides of the swordfish steaks with the herb mixture.
4. Grill swordfish for 4-5 minutes on each side or until the fish flakes easily with a fork.
5. Serve immediately with lemon wedges.

Nutrition Facts: Calories: 270 | Fat: 14g | Protein: 30g | Carbohydrates: 3g | Fiber: 1g

Roasted Vegetable and Quinoa Stuffed Eggplant

Prep: 20 mins | Cook: 40 mins | Serves: 4

Ingredients:
- 2 large eggplants, halved lengthwise
- 1 cup quinoa, rinsed
- 2 cups vegetable broth
- 1 red bell pepper, chopped
- 1 zucchini, chopped
- 1 red onion, chopped
- 3 cloves garlic, minced
- 1/4 cup olive oil
- Salt and pepper to taste
- 1/4 cup fresh parsley, chopped
- Feta cheese for garnish

Instructions:
1. Preheat the oven to 400°F (200°C).
2. Score the flesh of the eggplants with a knife, creating a grid pattern. Brush with olive oil and season with salt and pepper.
3. Place the eggplants cut side down on a baking sheet and roast for 20 minutes, or until soft.
4. Meanwhile, in a saucepan, bring the vegetable broth to a boil. Add the quinoa, cover, and reduce to a simmer for 15 minutes, or until cooked.
5. In a large skillet, heat the olive oil over medium heat. Add the bell pepper, zucchini, onion, and garlic. Cook for 10 minutes, or until softened.
6. Stir in the cooked quinoa and parsley. Season with salt and pepper.
7. Scoop out some of the flesh from the eggplants to create a boat. Chop the scooped-out eggplant and stir into the quinoa mixture.
8. Fill the eggplant boats with the quinoa mixture. Return to the oven and bake for an additional 20 minutes.
9. Garnish with feta cheese and serve.

Nutrition Facts: Calories: 350 | Fat: 16g | Protein: 9g | Carbohydrates: 44g | Fiber: 11g

Mediterranean Chickpea and Eggplant Curry

Prep: 10 mins | Cook: 25 mins | Serves: 4

Ingredients:
- 1 large eggplant, cubed
- 2 tablespoons olive oil
- 1 onion, diced
- 3 garlic cloves, minced
- 1 can (15 oz) chickpeas, drained and rinsed
- 1 can (14 oz) diced tomatoes
- 1 teaspoon cumin
- 1 teaspoon paprika
- 1/2 teaspoon turmeric
- 1/2 teaspoon cayenne pepper
- Salt and pepper to taste
- Fresh parsley for garnish
- Cooked rice for serving

Instructions:
1. In a large pan, heat olive oil over medium heat. Add eggplant and cook until browned and soft, about 7-10 minutes.
2. Add onion and garlic, and sauté until onion is translucent.
3. Stir in chickpeas, diced tomatoes, cumin, paprika, turmeric, cayenne pepper, salt, and pepper.
4. Bring to a simmer and let cook for 15 minutes, stirring occasionally.
5. Serve over rice and garnish with fresh parsley.

Nutrition Facts: Calories: 230 | Fat: 8g | Protein: 9g | Carbohydrates: 32g | Fiber: 10g

Greek-Style Baked Orzo with Chicken

Prep: 15 mins | Cook: 45 mins | Serves: 6

Ingredients:
- 2 tablespoons olive oil
- 4 boneless, skinless chicken thighs, cut into bite-sized pieces
- 1 onion, diced
- 3 garlic cloves, minced
- 1 1/2 cups orzo pasta
- 1 can (14 oz) diced tomatoes
- 3 cups chicken broth
- 1 teaspoon dried oregano
- 1 teaspoon dried basil
- Salt and pepper to taste
- 1 cup feta cheese, crumbled
- Fresh parsley for garnish

Instructions:
1. Preheat oven to 350°F (175°C).
2. In a large oven-safe pot or Dutch oven, heat olive oil over medium-high heat.
3. Add chicken and cook until browned on all sides.
4. Add onion and garlic, and sauté until onion is translucent.
5. Stir in orzo, diced tomatoes, chicken broth, oregano, basil, salt, and pepper.
6. Bring to a simmer, then cover and transfer to the oven.
7. Bake for 30 minutes or until orzo is cooked.
8. Stir in feta cheese and garnish with fresh parsley before serving.

Nutrition Facts: Calories: 360 | Fat: 12g | Protein: 23g | Carbohydrates: 40g | Fiber: 3g

Lemon Herb Mediterranean Chicken Salad

Prep: 15 mins | Cook: 10 mins | Serves: 4

Ingredients:
- 4 boneless, skinless chicken breasts
- 3 tablespoons olive oil
- Juice of 1 lemon
- 2 garlic cloves, minced
- 1 tablespoon fresh rosemary, chopped
- 1 tablespoon fresh thyme, chopped
- Salt and pepper to taste
- Mixed salad greens
- Cherry tomatoes, halved
- Cucumber, sliced
- Red onion, thinly sliced
- Feta cheese, crumbled
- Olives
- Lemon vinaigrette dressing

Instructions:
1. Preheat grill or grill pan to medium-high heat.
2. In a bowl, combine olive oil, lemon juice, garlic, rosemary, thyme, salt, and pepper.
3. Add chicken breasts and marinate for at least 15 minutes.
4. Grill chicken for 5-7 minutes on each side or until cooked through.
5. Slice chicken and serve over a bed of salad greens, tomatoes, cucumber, red onion, feta cheese, and olives.
6. Drizzle with lemon vinaigrette dressing before serving.

Nutrition Facts: Calories: 320 | Fat: 16g | Protein: 30g | Carbohydrates: 12g | Fiber: 3g

Stuffed Grape Leaves with Rice and Herbs (Dolma)

Prep: 30 mins | Cook: 40 mins | Serves: 6

Ingredients:
- 1 jar (16 oz) grape leaves, drained and rinsed
- 1 cup long-grain rice, rinsed
- 1 onion, finely chopped
- 3 tablespoons olive oil
- 3 tablespoons pine nuts
- 1/4 cup fresh parsley, chopped
- 2 tablespoons fresh dill, chopped
- 2 tablespoons fresh mint, chopped
- Juice of 2 lemons
- 1 1/2 cups vegetable broth
- Salt and pepper to taste
- Lemon slices for serving

Instructions:
1. In a large pot, bring a large amount of water to a boil. Blanch the grape leaves for 2-3 minutes. Drain and set aside.
2. In a skillet, heat the olive oil over medium heat. Add the onion and cook until translucent.
3. Add the pine nuts and rice, stirring for 2-3 minutes.
4. Stir in the parsley, dill, mint, lemon juice, salt, and pepper.
5. Place a grape leaf on a flat surface, vein side up. Place a teaspoon of the rice mixture near the stem end. Fold the sides in and roll up the leaf tightly.
6. Place the stuffed leaves seam side down in a large pot, packing them closely together.
7. Pour the vegetable broth over the grape leaves. Place a plate on top to keep them submerged.
8. Bring to a simmer, cover, and cook for 40 minutes.
9. Serve warm or at room temperature with lemon slices.

Nutrition Facts: Calories: 220 | Fat: 8g | Protein: 4g | Carbohydrates: 35g | Fiber: 3g

Baked Mediterranean Tilapia

Prep: 10 mins | Cook: 20 mins | Serves: 4

Ingredients:
- 4 tilapia fillets
- 2 tablespoons olive oil
- Juice of 1 lemon
- 1 teaspoon dried oregano
- 1 teaspoon dried basil
- 2 garlic cloves, minced
- Salt and pepper to taste
- 1 cup cherry tomatoes, halved
- 1/2 cup Kalamata olives, pitted and halved
- 1/4 cup red onion, thinly sliced
- 1/4 cup feta cheese, crumbled
- Fresh parsley for garnish

Instructions:
1. Preheat oven to 400°F (200°C).
2. Place tilapia fillets in a baking dish.
3. In a bowl, combine olive oil, lemon juice, oregano, basil, garlic, salt, and pepper.
4. Pour the mixture over the tilapia fillets, ensuring they are well coated.
5. Scatter cherry tomatoes, olives, and red onion around the fish.
6. Bake for 15-20 minutes or until the fish flakes easily with a fork.
7. Sprinkle feta cheese and fresh parsley over the top before serving.

Nutrition Facts: Calories: 280 | Fat: 15g | Protein: 30g | Carbohydrates: 8g | Fiber: 2g

Greek-Style Roasted Fish with Tomatoes

Prep: 10 mins | Cook: 25 mins | Serves: 4

Ingredients:
- 4 white fish fillets (such as cod or haddock)
- 2 tablespoons olive oil
- Juice of 1 lemon
- 4 garlic cloves, minced
- 1 teaspoon dried oregano
- Salt and pepper to taste
- 2 cups cherry tomatoes, halved
- 1/2 cup Kalamata olives, pitted
- Fresh basil for garnish

Instructions:
1. Preheat oven to 400°F (200°C).
2. Place fish fillets in a baking dish.
3. In a bowl, combine olive oil, lemon juice, garlic, oregano, salt, and pepper.
4. Pour the mixture over the fish fillets, ensuring they are well coated.
5. Scatter cherry tomatoes and olives around the fish.
6. Bake for 20-25 minutes or until the fish flakes easily with a fork.
7. Garnish with fresh basil before serving.

Nutrition Facts: Calories: 220 | Fat: 10g | Protein: 28g | Carbohydrates: 6g | Fiber: 2g

Mediterranean Bean and Barley Stew

Prep: 10 mins | Cook: 40 mins | Serves: 6

Ingredients:
- 1 tablespoon olive oil
- 1 onion, diced
- 3 garlic cloves, minced
- 1 carrot, diced
- 1 celery stalk, diced
- 1 cup barley, rinsed
- 1 can (15 oz) cannellini beans, drained and rinsed
- 1 can (14 oz) diced tomatoes
- 4 cups vegetable broth
- 1 teaspoon dried thyme
- Salt and pepper to taste
- Fresh parsley for garnish

Instructions:
1. In a large pot, heat olive oil over medium heat.
2. Add onion, garlic, carrot, and celery, and sauté until vegetables are soft.
3. Stir in barley, beans, tomatoes, vegetable broth, thyme, salt, and pepper.
4. Bring to a boil, then reduce heat and simmer for 30-40 minutes or until barley is cooked.
5. Serve hot, garnished with fresh parsley.

Nutrition Facts: Calories: 230 | Fat: 3g | Protein: 9g | Carbohydrates: 45g | Fiber: 10g

Pan-Seared Salmon with Mediterranean Salsa

Prep: 15 mins | Cook: 10 mins | Serves: 4

Ingredients:
- 4 salmon fillets
- Salt and pepper to taste
- 2 tablespoons olive oil
- 1 cup cherry tomatoes, chopped
- 1/2 cup cucumber, diced
- 1/4 cup red onion, finely chopped
- 1/4 cup Kalamata olives, chopped
- 2 tablespoons fresh parsley, chopped
- Juice of 1 lemon
- 1/4 cup feta cheese, crumbled

Instructions:
1. Season salmon fillets with salt and pepper.
2. Heat olive oil in a skillet over medium-high heat.
3. Add salmon fillets, skin side down, and cook for 4-5 minutes on each side or until cooked to your liking.
4. In a bowl, combine tomatoes, cucumber, red onion, olives, parsley, and lemon juice.
5. Serve salmon topped with Mediterranean salsa and crumbled feta.

Nutrition Facts: Calories: 320 | Fat: 20g | Protein: 29g | Carbohydrates: 6g | Fiber: 1g

Grilled Vegetables with Feta and Balsamic Glaze

Prep: 15 mins | Cook: 10 mins | Serves: 4

Ingredients:
- 2 zucchinis, sliced
- 2 red bell peppers, sliced
- 1 red onion, sliced
- 2 tablespoons olive oil
- Salt and pepper to taste
- 1/2 cup feta cheese, crumbled
- Balsamic glaze for drizzling
- Fresh basil for garnish

Instructions:
1. Preheat grill to medium-high heat.
2. Toss vegetables in olive oil, salt, and pepper.
3. Grill vegetables for 3-4 minutes on each side or until tender.
4. Serve vegetables topped with feta cheese, a drizzle of balsamic glaze, and fresh basil.

Nutrition Facts: Calories: 150 | Fat: 10g | Protein: 5g | Carbohydrates: 12g | Fiber: 3g

Baked Mediterranean Chicken with Lemon and Capers

Prep: 15 mins | Cook: 25 mins | Serves: 4

Ingredients:
- 4 boneless, skinless chicken breasts
- Salt and black pepper to taste
- 2 tablespoons olive oil
- Juice of 1 lemon
- 3 cloves garlic, minced
- 1 tablespoon capers, drained
- 1/2 cup chicken broth
- Fresh parsley, chopped (for garnish)

Instructions:
1. Preheat your oven to 375°F (190°C).
2. Season the chicken breasts with salt and pepper.
3. Heat the olive oil in an oven-safe skillet over medium-high heat.
4. Add the chicken breasts and sear on both sides until golden brown, about 3-4 minutes per side.
5. Remove the chicken from the skillet and set aside.
6. In the same skillet, add the garlic and sauté for 1 minute until fragrant.
7. Add the lemon juice, capers, and chicken broth. Stir to combine.
8. Return the chicken breasts to the skillet.
9. Transfer the skillet to the preheated oven and bake for 15-20 minutes, or until the chicken is cooked through.
10. Garnish with fresh parsley before serving.

Nutrition Facts: Calories: 220 | Fat: 9g | Protein: 30g | Carbohydrates: 4g | Fiber: 0g

Spaghetti Squash with Mediterranean Tomato Sauce

Prep: 15 mins | Cook: 40 mins | Serves: 4

Ingredients:
- 1 large spaghetti squash, halved lengthwise and seeds removed
- 2 tablespoons olive oil, divided
- Salt and black pepper to taste
- 1 onion, chopped
- 3 cloves garlic, minced
- 1 can (28 oz) crushed tomatoes
- 1 teaspoon dried oregano
- 1 teaspoon dried basil
- 1/2 cup Kalamata olives, pitted and chopped
- 1/4 cup capers, drained
- Fresh basil leaves for garnish

Instructions:
1. Preheat your oven to 400°F (200°C).
2. Brush the cut sides of the spaghetti squash with 1 tablespoon of olive oil and season with salt and pepper.
3. Place the squash cut side down on a baking sheet and roast for 30-40 minutes, or until tender.
4. While the squash is roasting, heat the remaining tablespoon of olive oil in a large skillet over medium heat.
5. Add the onion and garlic, and sauté until the onion is translucent, about 5 minutes.
6. Add the crushed tomatoes, oregano, and basil. Simmer for 15 minutes.
7. Stir in the olives and capers, and continue to simmer for an additional 5 minutes.
8. Once the spaghetti squash is done roasting, use a fork to scrape the flesh into strands.
9. Serve the spaghetti squash topped with the Mediterranean tomato sauce and garnished with fresh basil.

Nutrition Facts: Calories: 180 | Fat: 7g | Protein: 3g | Carbohydrates: 28g | Fiber: 6g

Greek Lamb Souvlaki with Tzatziki Sauce

Prep: 20 mins + marinating time | Cook: 10 mins | Serves: 4

Ingredients:
- 1 lb lamb, cut into 1-inch cubes
- 3 tablespoons olive oil
- Juice of 1 lemon
- 3 cloves garlic, minced
- 1 tablespoon dried oregano
- Salt and black pepper to taste
- 1 cup Greek yogurt
- 1 cucumber, grated and drained
- 2 tablespoons fresh dill, chopped
- 1 tablespoon white vinegar
- 4 pita breads, for serving

Instructions:
1. In a bowl, combine 2 tablespoons of olive oil, lemon

juice, 2 cloves of minced garlic, oregano, salt, and pepper.

2. Add the lamb cubes and toss to coat. Marinate for at least 30 minutes, or overnight for best results.
3. Preheat grill to medium-high heat.
4. Thread the marinated lamb cubes onto skewers.
5. Grill for 8-10 minutes, turning occasionally, until cooked to your desired doneness.
6. In another bowl, combine Greek yogurt, grated cucumber, remaining 1 clove of minced garlic, dill, and white vinegar. Mix well to make the tzatziki sauce.
7. Serve the lamb souvlaki with pita bread and a side of tzatziki sauce.

Nutrition Facts: Calories: 390 | Fat: 23g | Protein: 31g | Carbohydrates: 18g | Fiber: 2g

Mediterranean Vegetable Stew

Prep: 15 mins | Cook: 30 mins | Serves: 6

Ingredients:
- 2 tablespoons olive oil
- 1 onion, chopped
- 3 cloves garlic, minced
- 1 eggplant, diced
- 2 zucchinis, diced
- 1 bell pepper, diced
- 1 can (14 oz) diced tomatoes
- 1 can (15 oz) chickpeas, drained and rinsed
- 3 cups vegetable broth
- 1 teaspoon dried basil
- 1 teaspoon dried oregano
- Salt and black pepper to taste
- Fresh parsley for garnish

Instructions:
1. Heat the olive oil in a large pot over medium heat.
2. Add the onion and garlic, and sauté until the onion is translucent, about 5 minutes.
3. Add the eggplant, zucchinis, and bell pepper. Cook for an additional 5 minutes.
4. Stir in the diced tomatoes, chickpeas, vegetable broth, basil, oregano, salt, and pepper.
5. Bring to a boil, then reduce heat and simmer for 20 minutes.
6. Garnish with fresh parsley before serving.

Nutrition Facts: Calories: 150 | Fat: 5g | Protein: 6g | Carbohydrates: 23g | Fiber: 7g

Lemon and Garlic Roasted Chicken

Prep: 10 mins | Cook: 1 hr | Serves: 4

Ingredients:
- 1 whole chicken (about 4 lbs)
- 2 lemons, halved
- 1 whole head of garlic, halved
- 4 tablespoons olive oil
- Salt and black pepper to taste
- Fresh rosemary sprigs for garnish

Instructions:
1. Preheat your oven to 425°F (220°C).
2. Place the chicken in a roasting pan.

3. Squeeze the juice of 2 lemon halves over the chicken.
4. Place the squeezed lemon halves and the garlic halves inside the cavity of the chicken.
5. Rub the olive oil over the skin of the chicken and season with salt and pepper.
6. Roast for 1 hour, or until the chicken is cooked through and the skin is crispy.
7. Let the chicken rest for 10 minutes before carving.
8. Garnish with fresh rosemary and serve with the remaining lemon halves.

Nutrition Facts: Calories: 530 | Fat: 35g | Protein: 46g | Carbohydrates: 3g | Fiber: 1g

Mediterranean Eggplant and Chickpea Casserole

Prep Time: 20 minutes | Cook Time: 40 minutes | Serves: 6

Ingredients:
- 2 medium eggplants, cut into 1/2-inch slices
- Salt, to taste
- 3 tablespoons olive oil, divided
- 1 large onion, chopped
- 3 cloves garlic, minced
- 1 can (15 oz) chickpeas, drained and rinsed
- 1 can (14.5 oz) diced tomatoes
- 1 teaspoon dried oregano
- 1 teaspoon dried basil
- 1/2 cup crumbled feta cheese
- Fresh parsley, chopped, for garnish

Instructions:
1. Preheat your oven to 375°F (190°C).
2. Place the eggplant slices in a colander, sprinkle with salt, and let sit for 30 minutes to draw out bitterness. Rinse well and pat dry.
3. Heat 2 tablespoons of olive oil in a large skillet over medium heat. Add the eggplant slices in batches, cooking until browned on both sides. Remove from the skillet and set aside.
4. In the same skillet, add the remaining 1 tablespoon of olive oil, onion, and garlic. Sauté until the onion is translucent.
5. Add the chickpeas, diced tomatoes, oregano, and basil. Stir well and cook for another 5 minutes.
6. In a casserole dish, layer half of the eggplant slices, then half of the chickpea mixture, and repeat. Top with feta cheese.
7. Bake for 25-30 minutes, or until the casserole is heated through and the cheese is golden brown.
8. Garnish with fresh parsley before serving.

Nutrition Facts: Calories: 250 | Total Fat: 12g | Sodium: 300 mg | Carbohydrates: 30g

Grilled Octopus with Olive Oil and Lemon

Prep Time: 15 minutes + marinating time | Cook Time: 10 minutes | Serves: 4

Ingredients:
- 1 lb octopus, cleaned and tenderized
- 3 tablespoons olive oil, divided
- Juice of 1 lemon
- 3 cloves garlic, minced
- Salt and black pepper, to taste
- Lemon wedges, for serving
- Fresh parsley, chopped, for garnish

Instructions:
1. Place the octopus in a bowl with 2 tablespoons of olive oil, lemon juice, garlic, salt, and pepper. Toss to coat and let marinate for at least 30 minutes.
2. Preheat your grill to medium-high heat.
3. Grill the octopus for 4-5 minutes on each side, or until charred and cooked through.
4. Drizzle with the remaining 1 tablespoon of olive oil and season with additional salt and pepper if needed.
5. Serve with lemon wedges and garnish with fresh parsley.

Nutrition Facts: Calories: 200 | Fat: 10g | Protein: 20g | Carbohydrates: 5g | Fiber: 0g

Mediterranean Seafood Paella

Prep Time: 20 minutes | Cook Time: 40 minutes | Serves: 6

Ingredients:
- 2 tablespoons olive oil
- 1 onion, chopped
- 3 cloves garlic, minced
- 1 1/2 cups Arborio rice
- 1/4 teaspoon saffron threads (optional)
- 1 teaspoon paprika
- 1 can (14.5 oz) diced tomatoes
- 4 cups chicken or seafood broth
- 1 lb mixed seafood (such as shrimp, mussels, and squid), cleaned
- 1 cup frozen peas
- Salt and black pepper, to taste
- Lemon wedges, for serving
- Fresh parsley, chopped, for garnish

Instructions:
1. Heat the olive oil in a large paella pan or skillet over medium heat.
2. Add the onion and garlic, and sauté until the onion is translucent.
3. Add the rice, saffron (if using), and paprika. Stir well to coat the rice.
4. Pour in the diced tomatoes and broth. Bring to a simmer and cook for 20 minutes, stirring occasionally.
5. Add the seafood and peas, and continue to cook for another 10-15 minutes, or until the seafood is cooked through and the rice is tender.
6. Season with salt and pepper to taste.
7. Serve with lemon wedges and garnish with fresh parsley.

Nutrition Facts: Calories: 430 | Fat: 8g | Protein: 25g | Carbohydrates: 64g | Fiber: 4g

Greek-Style Stuffed Tomatoes (Gemista)

Prep Time: 20 minutes | Cook Time: 1 hour | Serves: 6

Ingredients:
- 6 large tomatoes
- Salt, to taste
- 3 tablespoons olive oil, divided
- 1 onion, chopped
- 3 cloves garlic, minced
- 1 cup Arborio rice
- 1/2 cup fresh parsley, chopped
- 1/2 cup fresh mint, chopped
- 1/4 cup pine nuts (optional)
- 1 1/2 cups tomato juice
- Fresh parsley, chopped, for garnish

Instructions:
1. Preheat your oven to 375°F (190°C).
2. Cut the tops off the tomatoes and set aside. Use a spoon to hollow out the insides, being careful not to break the skin. Sprinkle the insides with salt and invert onto paper towels to drain.
3. Heat 2 tablespoons of olive oil in a skillet over medium heat. Add the onion and garlic, and sauté until the onion is translucent.
4. Add the rice, parsley, mint, and pine nuts (if using), and cook for an additional 5 minutes, stirring frequently.
5. Fill each tomato with the rice mixture, then place the tops back on. Arrange in a baking dish.
6. Mix together the tomato juice and remaining 1 tablespoon of olive oil, and pour over the tomatoes.
7. Bake for 1 hour, or until the tomatoes are tender and the rice is cooked.
8. Garnish with fresh parsley before serving.

Nutrition Facts: Calories: 220 | Fat: 7g | Protein: 4g | Carbohydrates: 37g | Fiber: 4g

Baked Lemon and Herb Salmon

Prep Time: 10 minutes | Cook Time: 15 minutes | Serves: 4

Ingredients:
- 4 salmon fillets
- Juice and zest of 1 lemon
- 3 tablespoons olive oil
- 3 cloves garlic, minced
- 1 teaspoon dried oregano
- 1 teaspoon dried thyme
- Salt and black pepper, to taste
- Lemon slices, for garnish
- Fresh parsley, chopped, for garnish

Instructions:
1. Preheat your oven to 400°F (200°C).
2. In a small bowl, mix together the lemon juice and

zest, olive oil, garlic, oregano, thyme, salt, and pepper.
3. Place the salmon fillets in a baking dish, and pour the lemon-herb mixture over the top.
4. Bake for 12-15 minutes, or until the salmon flakes easily with a fork.
5. Serve garnished with lemon slices and fresh parsley.

Nutrition Facts: Calories: 345 | Fat: 24g | Protein: 30g | Carbohydrates: 2g | Fiber: 0g

Mediterranean Roasted Vegetable Orzo Salad

Prep Time: 20 minutes | Cook Time: 25 minutes | Serves: 6

Ingredients:
• 1 zucchini, chopped
• 1 red bell pepper, chopped
• 1 yellow bell pepper, chopped
• 1 red onion, chopped
• 2 tablespoons olive oil
• Salt and black pepper, to taste
• 2 cups orzo pasta
• 1/4 cup fresh basil, chopped
• 1/4 cup fresh parsley, chopped
• 1/4 cup feta cheese, crumbled
• 1/4 cup Kalamata olives, pitted and chopped
• Juice of 1 lemon
• 3 tablespoons extra virgin olive oil

Instructions:
1. Preheat your oven to 425°F (220°C).
2. Place the chopped vegetables on a baking sheet, drizzle with olive oil, and season with salt and black pepper. Toss to coat.
3. Roast in the preheated oven for 20-25 minutes, or until the vegetables are tender and slightly charred.
4. While the vegetables are roasting, bring a large pot of salted water to a boil. Cook the orzo according to package instructions until al dente. Drain and rinse under cold water to stop the cooking process.
5. In a large bowl, combine the cooked orzo, roasted vegetables, fresh basil, fresh parsley, feta cheese, and Kalamata olives.
6. In a small bowl, whisk together the lemon juice and extra virgin olive oil. Pour over the salad and toss to combine.
7. Season with additional salt and black pepper to taste, if necessary.
8. Serve chilled or at room temperature.

Nutrition Facts: Calories: 330 | Fat: 14g | Protein: 9g | Carbohydrates: 42g | Fiber: 3g

Grilled Chicken with Mediterranean Salsa

Prep Time: 15 minutes + marinating time | Cook Time: 15 minutes | Serves: 4

Ingredients:
• 4 boneless, skinless chicken breasts
• 3 tablespoons olive oil
• Juice of 1 lemon
• 3 cloves garlic, minced
• 1 teaspoon dried oregano
• Salt and black pepper, to taste
• 1 cup cherry tomatoes, halved
• 1/2 cup cucumber, diced
• 1/4 cup red onion, diced
• 1/4 cup Kalamata olives, pitted and chopped
• 1/4 cup feta cheese, crumbled
• 2 tablespoons fresh parsley, chopped
• 1 tablespoon extra virgin olive oil
• 1 tablespoon red wine vinegar

Instructions:
1. Place the chicken breasts in a resealable plastic bag.
2. In a small bowl, whisk together the olive oil, lemon juice, garlic, oregano, salt, and black pepper. Pour over the chicken, seal the bag, and marinate in the refrigerator for at least 30 minutes.
3. Preheat a grill or grill pan to medium-high heat.
4. Remove the chicken from the marinade and grill for 6-7 minutes on each side, or until the internal temperature reaches 165°F (74°C).
5. While the chicken is grilling, in a medium bowl, combine the cherry tomatoes, cucumber, red onion, Kalamata olives, feta cheese, fresh parsley, extra virgin olive oil, and red wine vinegar. Mix well.
6. Once the chicken is cooked, serve immediately topped with the Mediterranean salsa.

Nutrition Facts: Calories: 380 | Fat: 22g | Protein: 35g | Carbohydrates: 8g | Fiber: 2g

Greek-Style Beef Stew (Stifado)

Prep Time: 20 minutes | Cook Time: 2 hours | Serves: 6

Ingredients:
• 2 pounds beef stew meat, cut into chunks
• 3 tablespoons olive oil
• 2 large onions, sliced
• 5 cloves garlic, minced
• 1 cinnamon stick
• 5 whole cloves
• 2 bay leaves
• 1 can (14.5 oz) diced tomatoes
• 1/2 cup red wine
• 2 tablespoons red wine vinegar
• Salt and black pepper, to taste
• Fresh parsley, chopped, for garnish

Instructions:
1. In a large pot or Dutch oven, heat the olive oil over medium-high heat.
2. Add the beef chunks and brown on all sides. Remove from the pot and set aside.
3. In the same pot, add the sliced onions and garlic. Sauté until the onions are soft and golden.
4. Return the beef to the pot, along with the cinnamon stick, whole cloves, bay leaves, diced tomatoes, red wine, and red wine vinegar.
5. Bring to a simmer, reduce heat to low, cover, and simmer for 1.5-2 hours, or until the beef is tender.
6. Season with salt and black pepper to taste.
7. Serve hot, garnished with fresh parsley.

Nutrition Facts: Calories: 460 | Fat: 22g | Protein: 35g | Carbohydrates: 23g | Fiber: 3g

Mediterranean Vegan Shepherd's Pie

Prep Time: 25 minutes | Cook Time: 35 minutes | Serves: 6

Ingredients:
• 2 pounds potatoes, peeled and cut into chunks
• 3 tablespoons olive oil, divided
• Salt and black pepper, to taste
• 1 onion, diced
• 3 cloves garlic, minced
• 1 carrot, diced
• 1 zucchini, diced
• 1 red bell pepper, diced
• 1 can (15 oz) chickpeas, drained and rinsed
• 1 can (14.5 oz) diced tomatoes
• 2 teaspoons dried oregano
• 1 teaspoon cumin
• 1/2 cup almond milk
• Fresh parsley, chopped, for garnish

Instructions:
1. Preheat your oven to 400°F (200°C).
2. Place the potatoes in a large pot of salted water. Bring to a boil and cook until the potatoes are tender, about 15 minutes.
3. Meanwhile, heat 2 tablespoons of olive oil in a large skillet over medium heat. Add the onion and garlic, and sauté until the onion is translucent.
4. Add the carrot, zucchini, and red bell pepper. Cook for an additional 5 minutes, stirring occasionally.
5. Stir in the chickpeas, diced tomatoes, oregano, and cumin. Season with salt and black pepper. Cook for another 5 minutes, until the vegetables are tender.
6. Once the potatoes are cooked, drain and return to the pot. Add the almond milk and 1 tablespoon of olive oil. Mash until smooth and season with salt and black pepper.
7. Spread the vegetable mixture in an even layer in a baking dish. Top with the mashed potatoes, smoothing the top with a spatula.
8. Bake in the preheated oven for 20 minutes, or until the top is golden and the filling is bubbly.
9. Remove from the oven and let sit for 5 minutes before serving. Garnish with fresh parsley.

Nutrition Facts: Calories: 330 | Fat: 9g | Protein: 9g | Carbohydrates: 53g | Fiber: 10g

Lemon and Rosemary Roasted Lamb

Prep Time: 15 minutes + marinating time | Cook Time: 1 hour | Serves: 6

Ingredients:
• 1 boneless leg of lamb, about 3 pounds
• Juice and zest of 2 lemons
• 3 tablespoons olive oil
• 4 cloves garlic, minced
• 3 sprigs fresh rosemary, leaves stripped and chopped
• Salt and black pepper, to taste

Instructions:
1. In a small bowl, combine the lemon juice, lemon zest, olive oil, garlic, rosemary, salt, and black pepper.
2. Place the lamb in a large resealable plastic bag. Pour the marinade over the lamb, seal the bag, and refrigerate for at least 2 hours, or overnight for best results.
3. Preheat your oven to 400°F (200°C).
4. Remove the lamb from the marinade and place in a roasting pan. Pour any remaining marinade over the top.
5. Roast in the preheated oven for 1 hour, or until the internal temperature reaches 145°F (63°C) for medium-rare.
6. Remove from the oven and let rest for 10 minutes before slicing.
7. Serve the lamb sliced with your choice of sides. Enjoy!

Nutrition Facts: Calories: 410 | Fat: 28g | Protein: 35g | Carbohydrates: 2g | Fiber: 0g

Baked Falafel with Tahini Sauce

Prep Time: 15 minutes | Cook Time: 20 minutes | Serves: 4

Ingredients:
• 1 cup dry chickpeas (soaked overnight)
• 1 onion, chopped
• 3 cloves of garlic
• 1/4 cup fresh parsley
• 1/4 cup fresh cilantro
• 1 teaspoon ground cumin
• 1 teaspoon ground coriander
• Salt and pepper, to taste
• 1 teaspoon baking powder
• 3 tablespoons olive oil

Tahini Sauce:
• 1/2 cup tahini
• 3 tablespoons lemon juice
• 2 cloves garlic, minced
• Salt, to taste
• Water, as needed to thin

Instructions:
1. Preheat your oven to 375°F (190°C) and line a baking sheet with parchment paper.
2. In a food processor, combine soaked chickpeas, onion, garlic, parsley, cilantro, cumin, coriander, salt, pepper, and baking powder. Process until a coarse mixture forms.
3. Shape mixture into small balls or patties and place on the prepared baking sheet.
4. Brush the falafel with olive oil and bake for 20-25 minutes or until golden and crispy.
4. While the falafel is baking, prepare the tahini sauce by whisking together tahini, lemon juice, garlic, and salt. Add water as needed to reach your desired consistency.
5. Serve the baked falafel with tahini sauce drizzled on top or on the side for dipping.

Nutrition Facts: Calories: 340 | Fat: 20g | Protein: 12g |

Carbohydrates: 29g | Fiber: 7g

Mediterranean Cauliflower Rice with Grilled Veggies

Prep Time: 15 minutes | Cook Time: 15 minutes | Serves: 4

Ingredients:
• 1 large head of cauliflower, grated
• 2 bell peppers, sliced
• 1 zucchini, sliced
• 1 red onion, sliced
• 2 tablespoons olive oil
• Salt and pepper, to taste
• 1 teaspoon dried oregano
• 1 teaspoon dried basil
• 1/2 cup feta cheese, crumbled
• 1/4 cup fresh parsley, chopped

Instructions:
1. Preheat grill to medium-high heat.
2. Place the sliced bell peppers, zucchini, and red onion on a large tray and drizzle with olive oil.
3. Season with salt and pepper, and toss to coat.
4. Grill the veggies for 5-7 minutes on each side or until tender and slightly charred.
5. While the veggies are grilling, heat a large skillet over medium heat.
6. Add the grated cauliflower, dried oregano, dried basil, salt, and pepper. Cook for 5-7 minutes, stirring occasionally until the cauliflower is tender.
6. Remove from heat, and stir in the grilled veggies, feta cheese, and fresh parsley.
7. Serve immediately, garnished with additional fresh parsley if desired.

Nutrition Facts: Calories: 200 | Fat: 10g | Protein: 8g | Carbohydrates: 22g | Fiber: 7g

Greek Chicken and Potato Bake

Prep Time: 15 minutes | Cook Time: 1 hour | Serves: 4

Ingredients:
• 4 chicken thighs (bone-in, skin-on)
• 4 large potatoes, cut into wedges
• 3 tablespoons olive oil
• 4 cloves garlic, minced
• 2 teaspoons dried oregano
• Juice of 1 lemon
• Salt and pepper, to taste
• 1 cup chicken broth
• Fresh parsley, for garnish

Instructions:
1. Preheat your oven to 400°F (200°C).
2. In a large baking dish, place the chicken thighs and potato wedges.
3. In a small bowl, mix together the olive oil, minced garlic, dried oregano, lemon juice, salt, and pepper.
4. Pour the olive oil mixture over the chicken and potatoes, tossing to coat evenly.
5. Pour the chicken broth into the baking dish.

6. Bake for 50-60 minutes, or until the chicken is cooked through and the potatoes are tender.
7. Serve hot, garnished with fresh parsley.

Nutrition Facts: Calories: 540 | Fat: 29g | Protein: 31g | Carbohydrates: 41g | Fiber: 5g

Spiced Moroccan Chicken with Apricots and Almonds

Prep Time: 15 minutes | Cook Time: 45 minutes | Serves: 4

Ingredients:
• 4 chicken thighs (bone-in, skin-on)
• Salt and pepper, to taste
• 2 tablespoons olive oil
• 1 onion, sliced
• 3 cloves garlic, minced
• 1 teaspoon ground cumin
• 1 teaspoon ground coriander
• 1 teaspoon ground cinnamon
• 1 cup dried apricots, chopped
• 1/2 cup almonds, chopped
• 2 cups chicken broth
• Fresh cilantro, for garnish

Instructions:
1. Season the chicken thighs with salt and pepper.
2. Heat the olive oil in a large skillet over medium-high heat.
3. Add the chicken thighs, skin-side down, and cook for 5-7 minutes or until the skin is golden brown.
4. Flip the chicken and cook for an additional 5 minutes.
5. Remove the chicken from the skillet and set aside.
6. Add the onion and garlic to the skillet and sauté for 3-4 minutes.
7. Stir in the cumin, coriander, and cinnamon, and cook for another minute.
8. Add the apricots, almonds, and chicken broth. Bring to a simmer.
9. Return the chicken to the skillet, cover, and simmer for 25-30 minutes, or until the chicken is cooked through.
10. Serve the chicken topped with the apricot and almond mixture, garnished with fresh cilantro.

Nutrition Facts: Calories: 505 | Fat: 30g | Protein: 27g | Carbohydrates: 35g | Fiber: 5g

Mediterranean Quinoa Stuffed Bell Peppers

Prep Time: 15 minutes | Cook Time: 40 minutes | Serves: 4

Ingredients:
4 bell peppers, halved and seeds removed
1 cup quinoa, cooked
1 can (15 oz) chickpeas, drained and rinsed
1 cup cherry tomatoes, halved
1 cucumber, diced
1/4 cup red onion, finely chopped
1/4 cup feta cheese, crumbled
1/4 cup kalamata olives, pitted and chopped

3 tablespoons olive oil
Juice of 1 lemon
1 teaspoon dried oregano
Salt and pepper, to taste
Fresh parsley, for garnish

Instructions:
1. Preheat your oven to 375°F (190°C).
2. Place the bell pepper halves in a baking dish, cut-side up.
3. In a large bowl, combine the cooked quinoa, chickpeas, cherry tomatoes, cucumber, red onion, feta cheese, and kalamata olives.
4. In a small bowl, whisk together the olive oil, lemon juice, dried oregano, salt, and pepper.
5. Pour the dressing over the quinoa mixture, and stir to combine.
6. Spoon the quinoa mixture into the bell pepper halves.
7. Cover the baking dish with foil, and bake for 30 minutes.
8. Remove the foil, and bake for an additional 10 minutes, or until the peppers are tender.
9. Serve hot, garnished with fresh parsley.

Nutrition Facts: Calories: 360 | Fat: 15g | Protein: 11g | Carbohydrates: 48g | Fiber: 9g

Grilled Mediterranean Vegetarian Pizza

Prep Time: 15 minutes | **Cook Time:** 10 minutes | **Serves:** 4

Ingredients:
• 1 pound pizza dough, at room temperature
• 2 tablespoons olive oil
• 1 cup marinara sauce
• 1 cup shredded mozzarella cheese
• 1 cup cherry tomatoes, halved
• 1 red onion, thinly sliced
• 1 bell pepper, thinly sliced
• 1/2 cup Kalamata olives, pitted and sliced
• 1/2 cup feta cheese, crumbled
• Fresh basil leaves for garnish

Instructions:
1. Preheat your grill to medium-high heat.
2. On a floured surface, roll out the pizza dough to your desired thickness.
3. Brush one side of the dough with olive oil and place it oil-side-down on the grill. Cook for 2-3 minutes or until the bottom is golden brown.
4. Brush the top with more olive oil and flip the dough.
5. Quickly spread the marinara sauce over the dough, then sprinkle with mozzarella cheese.
6. Add the cherry tomatoes, red onion, bell pepper, and Kalamata olives.
7. Close the grill lid and cook for an additional 5-7 minutes or until the cheese is melted and the bottom is golden brown.
8. Remove from the grill, sprinkle with feta cheese and fresh basil.
9. Slice and serve immediately.

Nutrition Facts: Calories: 520 | Fat: 22g | Protein: 19g |

Carbohydrates: 65g | Fiber: 5g

Baked Branzino with Lemon and Herbs

Prep Time: 10 minutes | **Cook Time:** 20 minutes | **Serves:** 2

Ingredients:
• 2 whole branzino fish, cleaned and scaled
• 2 lemons, thinly sliced
• A bunch of fresh herbs (such as parsley, dill, or thyme)
• 2 tablespoons olive oil
• Salt and pepper to taste

Instructions:
1. Preheat your oven to 400°F (200°C).
2. Place the fish in a baking dish and season the cavities with salt and pepper.
3. Stuff the cavities with lemon slices and fresh herbs.
4. Drizzle the fish with olive oil and season the outside with more salt and pepper.
5. Bake for 20-25 minutes, or until the fish is cooked through and flakes easily with a fork.
6. Serve immediately with extra lemon slices on the side.

Nutrition Facts: Calories: 365 | Fat: 20g | Protein: 38g | Carbohydrates: 6g | Fiber: 1g

Mediterranean Shrimp Orzo Salad

Prep Time: 15 minutes | **Cook Time:** 10 minutes | **Serves:** 4

Ingredients:
• 1 cup orzo pasta
• 1 pound shrimp, peeled and deveined
• 2 tablespoons olive oil
• 1 cup cherry tomatoes, halved
• 1 cucumber, diced
• 1/4 cup red onion, finely chopped
• 1/2 cup Kalamata olives, pitted and sliced
• 1/2 cup feta cheese, crumbled
• Juice of 1 lemon
• 2 tablespoons fresh parsley, chopped
• Salt and pepper to taste

Instructions:
1. Cook the orzo according to package instructions. Drain and set aside to cool.
2. In a skillet, heat the olive oil over medium-high heat.
3. Add the shrimp and cook for 2-3 minutes on each side or until they are pink and cooked through. 4. Remove from heat.
5. In a large bowl, combine the cooked orzo, cooked shrimp, cherry tomatoes, cucumber, red onion, 6. Kalamata olives, and feta cheese.
7. Drizzle with lemon juice and sprinkle with fresh parsley. Toss to combine.
8. Season with salt and pepper to taste.
9. Serve immediately or refrigerate for later use.

Nutrition Facts: Calories: 429 | Fat: 16g | Protein: 33g | Carbohydrates: 41g | Fiber: 3g | Sugar: 4g

Greek-Style Baked Eggplant

Prep Time: 15 minutes | **Cook Time:** 45 minutes | **Serves:** 4

Ingredients:
- 2 large eggplants, sliced into 1/2-inch rounds
- 3 tablespoons olive oil
- Salt and pepper to taste
- 1 can (14 oz) diced tomatoes
- 3 cloves garlic, minced
- 1 teaspoon dried oregano
- 1/2 cup crumbled feta cheese
- Fresh parsley for garnish

Instructions:
1. Preheat your oven to 375°F (190°C).
2. Arrange the eggplant slices in a single layer on a baking sheet.
3. Brush both sides of the eggplant slices with olive oil and season with salt and pepper.
4. Bake for 20 minutes, or until the eggplant is tender.
5. While the eggplant is baking, in a saucepan over medium heat, combine the diced tomatoes, garlic, and oregano. Simmer for 10 minutes.
6. Remove the eggplant from the oven and top each slice with the tomato mixture.
7. Sprinkle with feta cheese.
8. Return to the oven and bake for an additional 15-20 minutes, or until the cheese is melted and golden brown.
9. Garnish with fresh parsley before serving.

Nutrition Facts: Calories: 220 | Fat: 13g | Cholesterol: 17mg | Carbohydrates: 24g | Fiber: 11g | Sugars: 14g | Protein: 7g

Mediterranean Chickpea Salad with Feta

Prep Time: 10 minutes | **Serves:** 4

Ingredients:
- 2 cans (15 oz each) chickpeas, drained and rinsed
- 1 cucumber, diced
- 1 red bell pepper, diced
- 1/4 red onion, finely chopped
- 1/2 cup Kalamata olives, pitted and sliced
- 1/2 cup feta cheese, crumbled
- 1/4 cup extra-virgin olive oil
- Juice of 1 lemon
- 2 teaspoons dried oregano
- Salt and pepper to taste
- Fresh parsley for garnish

Instructions:
1. In a large bowl, combine the chickpeas, cucumber, red bell pepper, red onion, Kalamata olives, and feta cheese.
2. In a small bowl, whisk together the olive oil, lemon juice, dried oregano, salt, and pepper.
3. Pour the dressing over the salad and toss to combine.
4. Garnish with fresh parsley before serving.
5. Serve immediately, or refrigerate for later use. Enjoy!

Nutrition Facts: Calories: 359 | Fat: 22g | Saturated

Fat: 5g | Cholesterol: 17mg | Sodium: 679mg | Carbohydrates: 33g | Fiber: 9g | Sugars: 6g | Protein: 13g

Lamb Tagine with Apricots and Almonds

Prep Time: 20 minutes | **Cook Time:** 2 hours | **Serves:** 4-6

Ingredients:
- 1.5 lbs lamb shoulder, cut into cubes
- 2 tablespoons olive oil
- 1 large onion, chopped
- 3 cloves garlic, minced
- 1 teaspoon ground cumin
- 1 teaspoon ground coriander
- 1 teaspoon ground cinnamon
- 1/2 teaspoon ground ginger
- 1/2 teaspoon cayenne pepper
- 2 cups beef or lamb broth
- 1 cup dried apricots
- 1/2 cup whole blanched almonds
- Salt and pepper to taste
- Fresh cilantro for garnish

Instructions:
1. In a large tagine or heavy-bottomed pot, heat the olive oil over medium-high heat.
2. Add the lamb cubes and brown on all sides. Remove the lamb from the pot and set aside.
3. Add the onion and garlic to the pot, and sauté until the onion is translucent.
4. Add the cumin, coriander, cinnamon, ginger, and cayenne pepper. Stir well to combine.
5. Return the lamb to the pot, and add the broth, apricots, and almonds.
6. Bring the mixture to a boil, then reduce the heat to low, cover, and simmer for 1.5 to 2 hours, or until the lamb is tender.
7. Season with salt and pepper to taste.
8. Garnish with fresh cilantro before serving.

Nutrition Facts: Calories: 440 | Fat: 25g | Saturated Fat: 6g | Cholesterol: 83mg | Sodium: 370mg | Carbohydrates: 27g | Fiber: 5g | Sugars: 16g | Protein: 30g

Grilled Halloumi and Vegetable Skewers

Prep Time: 15 minutes | **Cook Time:** 10 minutes | **Serves:** 4

Ingredients:
- 8 oz halloumi cheese, cut into cubes
- 1 zucchini, cut into chunks
- 1 red bell pepper, cut into chunks
- 1 yellow bell pepper, cut into chunks
- 1 red onion, cut into chunks
- Olive oil for brushing
- Lemon wedges for serving
- Fresh herbs (such as parsley or mint) for garnish

Instructions:

1. Preheat your grill to medium-high heat.
2. Thread the halloumi, zucchini, bell peppers, and red onion onto skewers.
3. Brush the vegetables and halloumi with olive oil.
4. Grill for 10-12 minutes, turning occasionally, until the vegetables are tender and the halloumi is golden brown.
5. Serve with lemon wedges and garnish with fresh herbs.

Nutrition Facts: Calories: 250 | Fat: 18g | Saturated Fat: 8g | Cholesterol: 35mg | Sodium: 810mg | Carbohydrates: 10g | Fiber: 2g | Sugars: 5g | Protein: 14g

Baked Grouper with Tomatoes and Olives

Prep Time: 10 minutes | Cook Time: 20 minutes | Serves: 4

Ingredients:
• 4 grouper fillets
• Salt and pepper to taste
• 2 tablespoons olive oil
• 2 cloves garlic, minced
• 1 pint cherry tomatoes, halved
• 1/2 cup Kalamata olives, pitted and sliced
• Fresh basil for garnish

Instructions:
1. Preheat your oven to 400°F (200°C).
2. Season the grouper fillets with salt and pepper.
3. In an ovenproof skillet, heat the olive oil over medium-high heat.
4. Add the grouper fillets and sear for 2-3 minutes on each side, or until golden brown.
5. Remove the fillets from the skillet and set aside.
6. Add the garlic to the skillet and sauté for 30 seconds, or until fragrant.
7. Add the cherry tomatoes and olives, and sauté for another 2-3 minutes.
8. Return the grouper fillets to the skillet.
9. Transfer the skillet to the oven and bake for 10-12 minutes, or until the fish is cooked through.
10. Garnish with fresh basil before serving.

Nutrition Facts: Calories: 280 | Fat: 15g | Saturated Fat: 2g | Cholesterol: 60mg | Sodium: 480mg | Carbohydrates: 7g | Fiber: 2g | Sugars: 4g | Protein: 29g

Mediterranean Lentil and Spinach Soup

Prep Time: 10 minutes | Cook Time: 30 minutes | Serves: 6

Ingredients:
• 1 tablespoon olive oil
• 1 onion, chopped
• 2 carrots, peeled and diced
• 3 cloves garlic, minced
• 1 teaspoon ground cumin
• 1/2 teaspoon ground coriander
• 1 cup dried lentils, rinsed and drained
• 8 cups vegetable broth

• 1 bay leaf
• 5 cups baby spinach
• Juice of 1 lemon
• Salt and pepper to taste
• Fresh parsley for garnish

Instructions:
1. In a large pot, heat the olive oil over medium-high heat.
2. Add the onion, carrots, and garlic. Sauté until the vegetables are softened, about 5 minutes.
3. Stir in the cumin and coriander.
4. Add the lentils, vegetable broth, and bay leaf. Bring to a boil.
5. Reduce the heat to low, cover, and simmer for 25 minutes, or until the lentils are tender.
6. Stir in the spinach and cook until wilted, about 2 minutes.
7. Add the lemon juice, salt, and pepper. Stir well.
8. Remove the bay leaf and discard.
9. Garnish with fresh parsley before serving.

Nutrition Facts: Calories: 210 | Fat: 3g | Sodium: 330mg | Carbohydrates: 35g | Fiber: 14g

Grilled Sardines with Lemon and Herbs

Prep Time: 10 minutes | Cook Time: 8 minutes | Serves: 4

Ingredients:
• 1 lb fresh sardines, cleaned and gutted
• Olive oil for brushing
• Salt and pepper to taste
• Juice of 2 lemons
• Fresh herbs (such as parsley, dill, or cilantro) for garnish
• Lemon wedges for serving

Instructions:
1. Preheat your grill to high heat.
2. Brush the sardines with olive oil and season with salt and pepper.
3. Grill the sardines for 3-4 minutes on each side, or until they are cooked through and the skin is crispy.
4. Remove from the grill and drizzle with lemon juice.
5. Garnish with fresh herbs.
6. Serve with lemon wedges.

Nutrition Facts: Calories: 190 | Fat: 12g | Cholesterol: 50mg | Sodium: 200mg | Carbohydrates: 1g

Chapter 6: Appetizers & Snacks

Hummus and Veggie Sticks

Prep Time: 10 minutes | Serves: 4

Ingredients:
- 2 cups hummus (store-bought or homemade)
- 1 cup baby carrots
- 1 cucumber, sliced
- 1 bell pepper, sliced
- 1 cup cherry tomatoes

Instructions:
1. Arrange the hummus in a serving bowl.
2. Place the baby carrots, cucumber slices, bell pepper slices, and cherry tomatoes around the hummus.
3. Serve immediately and enjoy!

Nutrition Facts: Calories: 250 | Total Fat: 14g | Sodium: 400mg | Carbohydrates: 26g

Greek Yogurt with Honey and Walnuts

Prep Time: 5 minutes | Serves: 1

Ingredients:
- 1 cup Greek yogurt
- 2 tablespoons honey
- 1/4 cup walnuts, chopped

Instructions:
1. Place the Greek yogurt in a serving bowl.
2. Drizzle the honey over the yogurt.
3. Sprinkle the chopped walnuts on top.
4. Serve immediately and enjoy!

Nutrition Facts: Calories: 320 | Total Fat: 15g | Cholesterol: 10mg | Carbohydrates: 35g

Olive Tapenade on Crostini

Prep Time: 15 minutes | Cook Time: 10 minutes | Serves: 8

Ingredients:
- 1 baguette, sliced
- 1 cup mixed olives, pitted
- 2 tablespoons capers
- 2 cloves garlic
- 2 tablespoons olive oil
- 1 lemon, juiced
- Fresh parsley, for garnish

Instructions:
1. Preheat the oven to 350°F (175°C).
2. Arrange the baguette slices on a baking sheet and toast in the oven for 5-7 minutes, or until golden brown.
3. In a food processor, combine the olives, capers, garlic, olive oil, and lemon juice. Pulse until the mixture is finely chopped.
4. Spread the olive tapenade over the toasted baguette slices.
5. Garnish with fresh parsley.
6. Serve immediately and enjoy!

Nutrition Facts: Calories: 180 | Total Fat: 9g | Carbohydrates: 21g

Mediterranean Stuffed Dates with Almonds

Prep Time: 15 minutes | Serves: 8

Ingredients:
- 16 Medjool dates, pitted
- 16 almonds
- 1/4 cup goat cheese
- 1 tablespoon honey
- Fresh mint leaves, for garnish

Instructions:
1. Make a slit in each date and stuff with an almond.
2. Dollop a small amount of goat cheese on top of each date.
3. Drizzle with honey.
4. Garnish with fresh mint leaves.
5. Serve immediately and enjoy!

Nutrition Facts: Calories: 150 | Total Fat: 2g | Cholesterol: 5mg | Carbohydrates: 33g

Baked Feta with Honey and Sesame Seeds

Prep Time: 5 minutes | Cook Time: 15 minutes | Serves: 4

Ingredients:
- 200g feta cheese block
- 2 tablespoons honey
- 1 tablespoon sesame seeds
- Olive oil, for drizzling
- Fresh thyme, for garnish

Instructions:
1. Preheat the oven to 400°F (200°C).
2. Place the feta cheese in a baking dish and drizzle with olive oil.
3. Bake in the preheated oven for 10-12 minutes, or until softened and slightly golden.
4. Remove from the oven and drizzle with honey.
5. Sprinkle with sesame seeds.
6. Garnish with fresh thyme.
7. Serve immediately and enjoy!

Nutrition Facts: Calories: 180 | Total Fat: 13g | Carbohydrates: 8g

Grilled Halloumi Cheese Bites

Prep Time: 10 mins | Cook Time: 5 mins | Serves: 4

Ingredients:
- 200g halloumi cheese, cut into bite-sized cubes
- 1 tablespoon olive oil
- A pinch of dried oregano
- A pinch of chili flakes (optional)

Instructions:
1. Preheat your grill or grill pan over medium-high heat.

2. Toss the halloumi cubes in olive oil, dried oregano, and chili flakes if using.
3. Place the halloumi on the grill, cooking for 2-3 minutes on each side or until golden brown and grill marks appear.
4. Remove from grill and serve immediately.

Nutrition Facts: Calories: 210 | Fat: 16g | Protein: 14g | Carbohydrates: 2g | Fiber: 0g

Caprese Skewers with Balsamic Glaze

Prep Time: 15 mins | Serves: 6

Ingredients:
- 24 cherry tomatoes
- 24 fresh basil leaves
- 24 mini mozzarella balls
- Balsamic glaze for drizzling
- Olive oil for drizzling
- Salt and pepper to taste

Instructions:
1. On small cocktail sticks, thread a cherry tomato, a basil leaf, and a mini mozzarella ball.
2. Arrange the skewers on a platter.
3. Drizzle with balsamic glaze and olive oil.
4. Season with salt and pepper.
5. Serve immediately or refrigerate until ready to serve.

Nutrition Facts: Calories: 80 | Fat: 5g | Protein: 5g | Carbohydrates: 4g | Fiber: 1g

Mediterranean Bruschetta with Tomato and Basil

Prep Time: 15 mins | Cook Time: 5 mins | Serves: 4

Ingredients:
- 1 baguette, sliced and toasted
- 2 large tomatoes, diced
- A handful of fresh basil, chopped
- 2 tablespoons olive oil
- Salt and pepper to taste
- 1 garlic clove, halved

Instructions:
1. In a bowl, combine the diced tomatoes, chopped basil, olive oil, salt, and pepper.
2. Rub the toasted baguette slices with the cut side of the garlic.
3. Top the bread with the tomato mixture.
4. Serve immediately.

Nutrition Facts: Calories: 150 | Fat: 5g | Protein: 3g | Carbohydrates: 22g | Fiber: 2g

Spicy Roasted Chickpeas

Prep Time: 5 mins | Cook Time: 25 mins | Serves: 4

Ingredients:
- 1 can (400g) chickpeas, drained and rinsed
- 1 tablespoon olive oil

- 1 teaspoon smoked paprika
- 1/2 teaspoon cayenne pepper
- Salt to taste

Instructions:
1. Preheat your oven to 400°F (200°C).
2. Toss the chickpeas in olive oil, smoked paprika, cayenne pepper, and salt.
3. Spread the chickpeas in a single layer on a baking sheet.
4. Roast for 20-25 minutes, or until crispy.
5. Remove from oven and let cool before serving.

Nutrition Facts: Calories: 120 | Fat: 4g | Protein: 5g | Carbohydrates: 17g | Fiber: 5g

Greek Yogurt Tzatziki Dip

Prep Time: 10 mins | Cook Time: 0 mins | Serves: 4

Ingredients:
- 1 cup Greek yogurt
- 1 cucumber, grated and squeezed to remove excess water
- 2 tablespoons fresh dill, chopped
- 2 garlic cloves, minced
- Juice of 1 lemon
- Salt and pepper to taste
- Olive oil for drizzling

Instructions:
1. In a bowl, combine Greek yogurt, grated cucumber, chopped dill, minced garlic, and lemon juice.
2. Season with salt and pepper to taste.
3. Drizzle with a bit of olive oil before serving.
4. Serve with pita bread or veggie sticks.

Nutrition Facts: Calories: 60 | Fat: 2g | Protein: 6g | Carbohydrates: 5g | Fiber: 0g

Marinated Olives and Feta

Prep Time: 10 minutes | Marinating Time: 1 hour | Serves: 4

Ingredients:
- 1 cup mixed olives
- 200g feta cheese, cubed
- 1/4 cup olive oil
- 2 cloves garlic, minced
- 1 tablespoon fresh rosemary, chopped
- 1 teaspoon red chili flakes
- Zest of 1 lemon

Instructions:
1. In a bowl, combine the olives, feta cheese, olive oil, garlic, rosemary, red chili flakes, and lemon zest.
2. Mix well to ensure the olives and feta are fully coated.
3. Cover and refrigerate for at least 1 hour to allow the flavors to marinate.
4. Bring to room temperature before serving.

Nutrition Facts: Calories: 250 | Total Fat: 22g | Cholesterol: 50mg | Carbohydrates: 6g

Stuffed Mini Bell Peppers with Goat Cheese

Prep Time: 20 minutes | Cook Time: 15 minutes | Serves: 4

Ingredients:
- 12 mini bell peppers, halved and seeds removed
- 200g goat cheese
- 2 tablespoons fresh basil, chopped
- 1 tablespoon olive oil
- Salt and pepper to taste
- Balsamic glaze for drizzling (optional)

Instructions:
1. Preheat the oven to 375°F (190°C).
2. In a bowl, mix together the goat cheese and fresh basil.
3. Stuff each bell pepper half with the goat cheese mixture.
4. Place the stuffed peppers on a baking sheet, drizzle with olive oil, and season with salt and pepper.
5. Bake for 15 minutes, or until the peppers are tender and the cheese is melted.
6. Drizzle with balsamic glaze before serving if desired.

Nutrition Facts: Calories: 220 | Total Fat: 16g | Cholesterol: 30mg | Carbohydrates: 10g

Mediterranean Sardine Toast

Prep Time: 10 minutes | Serves: 4

Ingredients:
- 4 slices whole grain bread, toasted
- 1 can (120g) sardines in olive oil, drained
- 1 tomato, sliced
- 1/4 red onion, thinly sliced
- 1 tablespoon fresh parsley, chopped
- Lemon wedges for serving

Instructions:
1. Place the toasted bread slices on plates.
2. Top each slice with sardines, tomato slices, and red onion.
3. Garnish with fresh parsley.
4. Serve with lemon wedges on the side.

Nutrition Facts: Calories: 180 | Total Fat: 9g | Cholesterol: 25mg | Carbohydrates: 14g

Lemon and Herb Marinated Mozzarella

Prep Time: 10 minutes | Marinating Time: 1 hour | Serves: 4

Ingredients:
- 200g fresh mozzarella balls
- Zest of 1 lemon
- Juice of 1 lemon
- 2 tablespoons olive oil
- 1 tablespoon fresh basil, chopped
- 1 tablespoon fresh oregano, chopped
- Salt and pepper to taste

Instructions:
1. In a bowl, combine the lemon zest, lemon juice, olive oil, basil, oregano, salt, and pepper.
2. Add the mozzarella balls and toss until well coated.
3. Cover and refrigerate for at least 1 hour to marinate.
4. Bring to room temperature before serving.

Nutrition Facts: Calories: 200 | Total Fat: 16g | Cholesterol: 30mg | Carbohydrates: 3g

Baba Ganoush with Pita Chips

Prep Time: 20 minutes | Cook Time: 45 minutes | Serves: 4

Ingredients:
- 1 large eggplant
- 2 tablespoons tahini
- 2 cloves garlic, minced
- Juice of 1 lemon
- 2 tablespoons olive oil
- Salt and pepper to taste
- 1 tablespoon fresh parsley, chopped
- Pita chips for serving

Instructions:
1. Preheat the oven to 400°F (200°C).
2. Pierce the eggplant with a fork and place it on a baking sheet.
3. Roast for 45 minutes, or until the eggplant is very soft.
4. Allow the eggplant to cool, then peel and place the flesh in a blender.
5. Add the tahini, garlic, lemon juice, and olive oil. Blend until smooth.
6. Season with salt and pepper to taste.
7. Transfer to a serving bowl and garnish with fresh parsley.
8. Serve with pita chips.

Nutrition Facts: Calories: 210 | Total Fat: 14g | Sodium: 310mg | Carbohydrates: 20g

Greek Spanakopita Bites

Prep Time: 15 minutes | Cook Time: 15 minutes | Serves: 4

Ingredients:
- 1 package (8 oz) frozen chopped spinach, thawed and drained
- 1/2 cup crumbled feta cheese
- 1/4 cup finely chopped red onion
- 2 cloves garlic, minced
- 1 tablespoon olive oil
- 1 teaspoon dried dill
- Salt and pepper to taste
- 1 package mini phyllo pastry shells

Instructions:
1. Preheat the oven to 375°F (190°C).
2. In a skillet, heat the olive oil over medium heat. Add the red onion and garlic, sautéing until aromatic and soft.
3. Stir in the spinach, feta, dill, salt, and pepper, mixing until the ingredients are well combined.
4. Spoon the spinach mixture into the mini phyllo shells,

filling them evenly.
5. Place the filled shells on a baking sheet and bake for 12-15 minutes, until the edges of the shells are golden brown.
6. Serve warm.

Nutrition Facts: Calories: 220 | Total Fat: 14g | Saturated Fat: 4g | Cholesterol: 20mg | Sodium: 320mg | Carbohydrates: 18g

Tomato and Cucumber Salad with Feta

Prep Time: 10 minutes | Serves: 4

Ingredients:
• 3 medium tomatoes, diced
• 1 cucumber, diced
• 1/2 cup crumbled feta cheese
• 1/4 cup chopped red onion
• 1/4 cup chopped fresh parsley
• 3 tablespoons olive oil
• 1 tablespoon red wine vinegar
• Salt and pepper to taste

Instructions:
1. In a large bowl, combine the tomatoes, cucumber, feta, red onion, and parsley.
2. Drizzle with olive oil and red wine vinegar, tossing to combine.
3. Season with salt and pepper to taste.
4. Chill in the refrigerator for 10 minutes before serving.

Nutrition Facts: Calories: 180 | Total Fat: 15g | Cholesterol: 20mg | Sodium: 320mg | Carbohydrates: 8g

Roasted Red Pepper Hummus

Prep Time: 10 minutes | Serves: 4

Ingredients:
• 1 can (15 oz) chickpeas, drained and rinsed
• 1 jar (12 oz) roasted red peppers, drained
• 3 tablespoons tahini
• 2 cloves garlic
• Juice of 1 lemon
• 3 tablespoons olive oil
• Salt and pepper to taste
• 1 tablespoon chopped fresh parsley for garnish

Instructions:
1. In a blender or food processor, combine the chickpeas, roasted red peppers, tahini, garlic, and lemon juice.
2. Pulse until smooth, gradually adding the olive oil until the desired consistency is reached.
3. Season with salt and pepper to taste.
4. Transfer to a serving bowl and garnish with chopped parsley.
5. Serve with pita bread or vegetable sticks.
Nutrition Facts: Calories: 210 | Total Fat: 12g | Sodium: 590mg | Total Carbohydrates: 22g

Olive and Tomato Caprese Salad

Prep Time: 10 minutes | Serves: 4

Ingredients:
• 4 ripe tomatoes, sliced
• 1/2 cup pitted Kalamata olives
• 1/2 cup fresh mozzarella cheese, sliced
• 1/4 cup fresh basil leaves
• 3 tablespoons olive oil
• Balsamic glaze for drizzling
• Salt and pepper to taste

Instructions:
1. Arrange the tomato slices, mozzarella slices, and olives on a platter.
2. Scatter the fresh basil leaves over the top.
3. Drizzle with olive oil and balsamic glaze.
4. Season with salt and pepper to taste.
5. Serve immediately.

Nutrition Facts: Calories: 210 | Total Fat: 15g | Saturated Fat: 4g | Cholesterol: 20mg | Sodium: 410mg | Carbohydrates: 12g

Lemon Garlic Labneh

Prep Time: 10 minutes + overnight draining | Serves: 4

Ingredients:
• 2 cups plain Greek yogurt
• 2 cloves garlic, minced
• Zest of 1 lemon
• Juice of 1/2 lemon
• 2 tablespoons olive oil
• Salt and pepper to taste

Instructions:
1. Line a strainer with a clean kitchen cloth and place it over a bowl.
2. Pour the Greek yogurt into the strainer, cover with plastic wrap, and let it drain in the refrigerator overnight to thicken.
3. The next day, transfer the thickened yogurt to a bowl.
4. Add the minced garlic, lemon zest, lemon juice, and olive oil, stirring to combine.
5. Season with salt and pepper to taste.
6. Serve with pita chips or fresh vegetables.

Nutrition Facts: Calories: 180 | Total Fat: 10g | Cholesterol: 5mg | Sodium: 60mg | Carbohydrates: 12g

Fig and Almond Energy Bites

Prep Time: 10 minutes | Serves: 4

Ingredients:
• 1 cup dried figs
• 1 cup raw almonds
• 1 tablespoon chia seeds
• 1 tablespoon honey
• A pinch of salt

Instructions:

1. In a food processor, combine the dried figs, raw almonds, chia seeds, honey, and a pinch of salt.
2. Pulse until the mixture is finely chopped and starts to clump together.
3. Take small amounts of the mixture and roll into bite-sized balls.
4. Place the energy bites on a plate and refrigerate for 30 minutes to set.
5. Serve and enjoy!

Nutrition Facts: Calories: 210 | Total Fat: 11g | Sodium: 10mg | Carbohydrates: 28g | Fiber: 5g

Greek Yogurt and Berry Parfait

Prep Time: 5 minutes | Serves: 4

Ingredients:
• 2 cups Greek yogurt
• 1 cup mixed berries (strawberries, blueberries, raspberries)
• 2 tablespoons honey
• 1/2 cup granola

Instructions:
1. In serving glasses, layer Greek yogurt, mixed berries, and granola.
2. Drizzle honey over the top of each parfait.
3. Serve immediately and enjoy!

Nutrition Facts: Calories: 180 | Total Fat: 2g | Cholesterol: 5mg | Sodium: 50mg | Carbohydrates: 33g

Mediterranean Falafel Balls

Prep Time: 15 minutes | Cook Time: 10 minutes | Serves: 4

Ingredients:
• 1 can (15 oz) chickpeas, drained and rinsed
• 1/2 cup chopped fresh parsley
• 1/2 cup chopped red onion
• 3 cloves garlic, minced
• 1 teaspoon ground cumin
• 1 teaspoon ground coriander
• Salt and pepper to taste
• Oil for frying

Instructions:
1. In a food processor, combine chickpeas, parsley, red onion, garlic, cumin, coriander, salt, and pepper. Pulse until well combined.
2. Form the mixture into small balls and flatten slightly to form patties.
3. Heat oil in a frying pan over medium heat. Fry the falafel balls in batches until golden brown and cooked through, about 4-5 minutes per side.
4. Drain on paper towels and serve hot.

Nutrition Facts: Calories: 220 | Total Fat: 11g | Sodium: 320mg | Carbohydrates: 24g

Pita Chips with Za'atar Spice

Prep Time: 5 minutes | Cook Time: 10 minutes | Serves: 4

Ingredients:
• 4 pita bread rounds
• 3 tablespoons olive oil
• 2 tablespoons za'atar spice
• Salt to taste

Instructions:
1. Preheat oven to 350°F (175°C).
2. Cut each pita round into 8 wedges and place on a baking sheet.
3. Brush each wedge with olive oil and sprinkle with za'atar spice and salt.
4. Bake for 10 minutes or until the chips are crispy.
5. Serve immediately and enjoy!

Nutrition Facts: Calories: 200 | Total Fat: 10g | Sodium: 320mg | Carbohydrates: 24g | Fiber: 3g

Stuffed Grape Leaves (Dolmas)

Prep Time: 20 minutes | Cook Time: 40 minutes | Serves: 4

Ingredients:
• 1 jar (16 oz) grape leaves in brine, drained and rinsed
• 1 cup cooked rice
• 1/2 cup pine nuts
• 1/2 cup chopped fresh dill
• 1/2 cup chopped fresh mint
• 3 tablespoons olive oil
• Juice of 1 lemon
• Salt and pepper to taste

Instructions:
1. In a bowl, combine the cooked rice, pine nuts, dill, mint, olive oil, lemon juice, salt, and pepper.
2. Lay a grape leaf flat on a work surface, shiny side down.
3. Place a spoonful of the rice mixture near the stem end of the leaf.
4. Fold in the sides and roll up the leaf to encase the filling. Repeat with the remaining leaves and filling.
5. Place the stuffed grape leaves in a single layer in a large skillet.
6. Add enough water to just cover the grape leaves, and bring to a simmer over medium heat.
7. Cover and cook for 30-40 minutes, or until the grape leaves are tender.
8. Serve warm or at room temperature.

Nutrition Facts: Calories: 220 | Total Fat: 14g | Sodium: 660mg | Carbohydrates: 22g | Fiber: 3g

Mediterranean Eggplant Dip

Prep Time: 15 minutes | Cook Time: 30 minutes | Serves: 4

Ingredients:
- 1 large eggplant
- 2 cloves garlic, minced
- 2 tablespoons tahini
- Juice of 1 lemon
- 2 tablespoons chopped fresh parsley
- 2 tablespoons olive oil
- Salt and pepper to taste

Instructions:
1. Preheat oven to 400°F (200°C).
2. Pierce the eggplant with a fork several times. Place on a baking sheet and roast for 30 minutes or until soft.
3. Allow the eggplant to cool, then peel and place the flesh in a food processor.
4. Add garlic, tahini, lemon juice, parsley, olive oil, salt, and pepper. Pulse until smooth.
5. Transfer to a bowl and serve with pita bread or vegetable sticks.

Nutrition Facts: Calories: 140 | Total Fat: 10g | Sodium: 60mg, | Carbohydrates: 12g | Fiber: 5g

Roasted Almonds with Rosemary and Sea Salt

Prep Time: 5 minutes | Cook Time: 10 minutes | Serves: 4

Ingredients:
- 1 cup raw almonds
- 2 tablespoons olive oil
- 2 teaspoons fresh rosemary, chopped
- Sea salt to taste

Instructions:
1. Preheat oven to 350°F (175°C).
2. In a bowl, mix almonds with olive oil, rosemary, and sea salt.
3. Spread the almonds on a baking sheet in a single layer.
4. Bake for 10 minutes or until golden brown.
5. Allow to cool before serving.

Nutrition Facts: Calories: 210 | Total Fat: 18g | Sodium: 180mg | Carbohydrates: 7g | Fiber: 4g

Grilled Pita with Olive Oil and Za'atar

Prep Time: 5 minutes | Cook Time: 5 minutes | Serves: 4

Ingredients:
- 4 pita bread rounds
- 1/4 cup olive oil
- 2 tablespoons za'atar spice

Instructions:
1. Preheat grill to medium-high heat.

2. Brush each pita bread with olive oil and sprinkle with za'atar spice.
3. Grill for 2-3 minutes on each side until lightly charred and crispy.
4. Serve warm.

Nutrition Facts: Calories: 250 | Total Fat: 14g | Sodium: 320mg | Carbohydrates: 28g | Fiber: 1g

Mediterranean Guacamole with Pomegranate Seeds

Prep Time: 15 minutes | Serves: 4

Ingredients:
- 2 ripe avocados, peeled and pitted
- Juice of 1 lemon
- 1/2 cup pomegranate seeds
- 2 tablespoons chopped fresh cilantro
- Salt to taste

Instructions:
1. In a bowl, mash the avocados with lemon juice until smooth.
2. Stir in pomegranate seeds, cilantro, and salt.
3. Transfer to a serving dish and enjoy with tortilla chips or pita bread.

Nutrition Facts: Calories: 210 | Total Fat: 15g | Sodium: 10mg | Carbohydrates: 18g | Fiber: 7g

Feta and Watermelon Skewers

Prep Time: 10 minutes | Serves: 4

Ingredients:
- 1 cup watermelon cubes
- 1 cup feta cheese cubes
- Fresh mint leaves for garnish

Instructions:
1. On small skewers, alternately thread watermelon and feta cubes.
2. Garnish with fresh mint leaves.
3. Serve chilled as a refreshing appetizer.

Nutrition Facts: Calories: 110 | Total Fat: 6g | Cholesterol: 25mg | Sodium: 270mg | Carbohydrates: 9g

Tomato Bruschetta with Ricotta

Prep Time: 10 minutes | Cook Time: 5 minutes | Serves: 4

Ingredients:
- 1 baguette, sliced
- 2 cups cherry tomatoes, halved
- 1 cup ricotta cheese
- 1/4 cup fresh basil, chopped
- 2 tablespoons balsamic glaze
- Salt and pepper to taste
- Olive oil for drizzling

Instructions:
1. Preheat oven to 350°F (175°C).

2. Arrange baguette slices on a baking sheet and drizzle with olive oil.
3. Toast in the oven for 5 minutes or until golden and crisp.
4. In a bowl, combine tomatoes, basil, salt, and pepper.
5. Spread ricotta cheese on each baguette slice.
6. Top with tomato mixture and drizzle with balsamic glaze.
7. Serve immediately and enjoy!

Nutrition Facts: Calories: 310 | Total Fat: 9g | Cholesterol: 20mg | Sodium: 470mg | Carbohydrates: 44g

Greek Yogurt and Granola

Prep Time: 5 minutes | Serves: 4

Ingredients:
• 4 cups Greek yogurt
• 2 cups granola
• 1 cup mixed berries
• Honey for drizzling

Instructions:
1. In each serving bowl, layer Greek yogurt and granola.
2. Top with mixed berries and a drizzle of honey.
3. Serve immediately and enjoy!

Nutrition Facts: Calories: 420 | Total Fat: 8g | Cholesterol: 10mg | Sodium: 100mg | Carbohydrates: 64g

Mediterranean Veggie Mini Frittatas

Prep Time: 15 minutes | Cook Time: 20 minutes | Serves: 4

Ingredients:
• 6 large eggs
• 1/2 cup milk
• 1 cup spinach, chopped
• 1/2 cup cherry tomatoes, halved
• 1/2 cup feta cheese, crumbled
• Salt and pepper to taste
• Olive oil for greasing

Instructions:
1. Preheat oven to 350°F (175°C).
2. In a bowl, whisk together eggs, milk, salt, and pepper.
3. Stir in spinach, cherry tomatoes, and feta cheese.
4. Grease a muffin tin with olive oil and fill each cup with the egg mixture.
5. Bake for 20 minutes or until the frittatas are set and golden on top.
6. Allow to cool for a few minutes before serving.

Nutrition Facts: Calories: 200 | Total Fat: 14g | Cholesterol: 285mg | Sodium: 370mg | Carbohydrates: 6g

Roasted Mediterranean Vegetables

Prep Time: 10 minutes | Cook Time: 20 minutes | Serves: 4

Ingredients:
• 1 zucchini, sliced
• 1 bell pepper, chopped
• 1 red onion, chopped
• 1 eggplant, chopped
• 2 tablespoons olive oil
• Salt and pepper to taste
• 1 teaspoon dried oregano

Instructions:
1. Preheat oven to 400°F (200°C).
2. On a baking sheet, toss vegetables with olive oil, salt, pepper, and oregano.
3. Roast for 20 minutes or until vegetables are tender and caramelized.
4. Serve warm as a side dish.

Nutrition Facts: Calories: 110 | Total Fat: 7g | Sodium: 10mg | Carbohydrates: 12g | Fiber: 4g

Olive and Artichoke Tapenade

Prep Time: 10 minutes | Serves: 4

Ingredients:
• 1 cup pitted olives, mixed varieties
• 1/2 cup canned artichoke hearts, drained
• 2 cloves garlic, minced
• Juice of 1 lemon
• 2 tablespoons capers, drained
• 2 tablespoons olive oil
• Salt and pepper to taste

Instructions:
1. In a food processor, combine olives, artichoke hearts, garlic, lemon juice, capers, and olive oil.
2. Pulse until the mixture is finely chopped but still has some texture.
3. Season with salt and pepper to taste.
4. Transfer to a serving bowl and enjoy with crackers or crusty bread.

Nutrition Facts: Calories: 120 | Total Fat: 10g | Sodium: 720mg | Carbohydrates: 7g | Fiber: 3g

Grilled Shrimp with Lemon and Herbs

Prep Time: 15 minutes | Cook Time: 5 minutes | Serves: 4

Ingredients:
• 1 pound large shrimp, peeled and deveined
• 3 tablespoons olive oil
• Juice and zest of 1 lemon
• 3 cloves garlic, minced
• 1 tablespoon fresh parsley, chopped
• 1 tablespoon fresh basil, chopped
• Salt and pepper to taste

Instructions:

1. In a bowl, combine olive oil, lemon juice and zest, garlic, parsley, basil, salt, and pepper.
2. Add the shrimp and toss to coat. Let marinate for at least 30 minutes.
3. Preheat grill to medium-high heat.
4. Grill shrimp for 2-3 minutes per side or until they are opaque and cooked through.
5. Serve immediately with a sprinkle of fresh herbs and a squeeze of lemon juice if desired.

Nutrition Facts: Calories: 210 | Total Fat: 10g | Cholesterol: 230mg | Sodium: 310mg | Carbohydrates: 3g

Mediterranean Cheese and Charcuterie Board

Prep Time: 20 minutes | Serves: 6-8

Ingredients:
• Various cheeses (feta, brie, manchego)
• Various charcuterie meats (salami, prosciutto)
• Olives
• Nuts (almonds, walnuts)
• Fresh and dried fruits
• Crackers and/or bread

Instructions:
1. Arrange the cheeses, meats, olives, nuts, fruits, and crackers on a large board.
2. Serve with small knives for the cheeses and forks for the olives.

Nutrition Facts: Calories: 450 | Total Fat: 35g | Cholesterol: 80mg | Sodium: 900mg | Total Carbohydrates: 12g

Greek Salad Cups with Hummus

Prep Time: 15 minutes | Serves: 4

Ingredients:
• 1 cup hummus
• 1 cup cherry tomatoes, halved
• 1 cup cucumber, diced
• 1/2 cup feta cheese, crumbled
• 1/4 cup red onion, finely chopped
• 1/4 cup Kalamata olives, pitted and sliced
• Fresh parsley for garnish

Instructions:
1. In serving cups, layer hummus, tomatoes, cucumber, feta, red onion, and olives.
2. Garnish with fresh parsley.
3. Serve with pita chips or veggies for dipping.

Nutrition Facts: Calories: 210 | Total Fat: 12g | Cholesterol: 15mg | Sodium: 610mg | Carbohydrates: 18g

Quinoa Tabbouleh Salad

Prep Time: 20 minutes | Cook Time: 15 minutes (for quinoa) | Serves: 4

Ingredients:
• 1 cup quinoa, uncooked
• 2 cups water
• 1 cup fresh parsley, chopped
• 1/2 cup fresh mint, chopped
• 1 cup tomatoes, diced
• 1 cup cucumber, diced
• 3 tablespoons olive oil
• Juice of 1 lemon
• Salt and pepper to taste

Instructions:
1. Rinse quinoa under cold water.
2. Bring 2 cups of water to a boil, add quinoa, reduce heat, cover, and simmer for 15 minutes or until water is absorbed.
3. Fluff quinoa with a fork and let it cool.
4. In a large bowl, combine quinoa, parsley, mint, tomatoes, and cucumber.
5. In a small bowl, whisk together olive oil, lemon juice, salt, and pepper.
6. Pour the dressing over the salad and toss to combine.
7. Chill in the refrigerator for at least 30 minutes before serving.

Nutrition Facts: Calories: 250 | Total Fat: 10g | Total Carbohydrates: 34g | Fiber: 5g

Baked Zucchini Chips with Tzatziki Sauce

Prep Time: 15 minutes | Cook Time: 20 minutes | Serves: 4

Ingredients:
• 2 large zucchinis, sliced into thin rounds
•
•
• 1 tablespoon olive oil
• Salt and pepper to taste
• 1 cup Greek yogurt
• 1/2 cucumber, grated
• 2 cloves garlic, minced
• 1 tablespoon fresh dill, chopped
• Juice of 1/2 lemon

Instructions:
1. Preheat oven to 425°F (220°C).
2. Toss zucchini rounds with olive oil, salt, and pepper.
3. Spread in a single layer on a baking sheet.
4. Bake for 20 minutes or until crispy and golden brown.
5. Meanwhile, prepare tzatziki sauce by combining Greek yogurt, grated cucumber, garlic, dill, and lemon juice in a bowl.
6. Serve zucchini chips hot with tzatziki sauce for dipping.

Nutrition Facts: Calories: 120 | Total Fat: 5g | Cholesterol: 5mg | Sodium: 40m, | Carbohydrates: 12g

Mediterranean Chickpea Salad

Prep Time: 10 minutes | Serves: 4

Ingredients:
- 1 can (15 ounces) chickpeas, drained and rinsed
- 1 cup cherry tomatoes, halved
- 1 cup cucumber, diced
- 1/2 cup red onion, finely chopped
- 1/2 cup feta cheese, crumbled
- 1/4 cup Kalamata olives, pitted and sliced
- 1/4 cup fresh parsley, chopped
- 3 tablespoons olive oil
- Juice of 1 lemon
- Salt and pepper to taste

Instructions:
1. In a large bowl, combine chickpeas, tomatoes, cucumber, red onion, feta cheese, olives, and parsley.
2. In a small bowl, whisk together olive oil, lemon juice, salt, and pepper.
3. Pour the dressing over the salad and toss to combine.
4. Serve immediately, or chill in the refrigerator for 30 minutes before serving.

Nutrition Facts: Calories: 250 | Total Fat: 12g | Cholesterol: 15mg | Carbohydrates: 28g

Grilled Vegetable Skewers

Prep Time: 15 minutes (plus marinating time) | Cook Time: 10 minutes | Serves: 4

Ingredients:
- 1 zucchini, cut into chunks
- 1 red bell pepper, cut into chunks
- 1 yellow bell pepper, cut into chunks
- 1 red onion, cut into chunks
- 8 cherry tomatoes
- 1/4 cup olive oil
- 3 cloves garlic, minced
- 1 teaspoon dried oregano
- Salt and pepper to taste

Instructions:
1. Preheat grill to medium-high heat.
2. Thread the vegetables onto skewers, alternating types.
3. In a small bowl, combine olive oil, garlic, oregano, salt, and pepper.
4. Brush the marinade over the vegetables.
5. Grill for 10-12 minutes, turning occasionally, until vegetables are tender and slightly charred.
6. Serve immediately.

Nutrition Facts: Calories: 150 | Total Fat: 10g | Carbohydrates: 14g | Fiber: 3g

Feta and Spinach Stuffed Mushrooms

Prep Time: 15 minutes | Cook Time: 20 minutes | Serves: 4

Ingredients:
- 16 large mushrooms, stems removed
- 2 cups fresh spinach, chopped
- 1/2 cup feta cheese, crumbled
- 2 cloves garlic, minced
- 2 tablespoons olive oil
- Salt and pepper to taste

Instructions:
1. Preheat oven to 375°F (190°C).
2. In a skillet, heat 1 tablespoon of olive oil over medium heat.
3. Add garlic and spinach, sautéing until spinach is wilted.
4. Remove from heat and stir in feta cheese.
5. Place mushroom caps on a baking sheet, drizzle with remaining olive oil, and season with salt and pepper.
6. Stuff each mushroom cap with the spinach and feta mixture.
7. Bake for 20 minutes, or until mushrooms are tender.
8. Serve immediately.

Nutrition Facts: Calories: 130 | Total Fat: 9g | Cholesterol: 15mg | Sodium: 310mg | Total Carbohydrates: 7g

Lemon and Mint Yogurt Dip

Prep Time: 5 minutes | Serves: 4

Ingredients:
- 1 cup Greek yogurt
- Juice and zest of 1 lemon
- 1/4 cup fresh mint, chopped
- 1 clove garlic, minced
- Salt and pepper to taste

Instructions:
1. In a bowl, combine Greek yogurt, lemon juice and zest, mint, garlic, salt, and pepper.
2. Stir until well combined.
3. Chill in the refrigerator for at least 30 minutes before serving.
4. Serve with fresh vegetables, pita chips, or as a sauce for grilled meats.

Nutrition Facts: Calories: 60 | Total Fat: 2g | Cholesterol: 5mg | Sodium: 30mg | Carbohydrates: 5g

Greek Yogurt and Fig Compote

Prep Time: 10 minutes | Cook Time: 10 minutes | Serves: 4

Ingredients:
• 1 cup Greek yogurt
• 6 fresh figs, quartered
• 2 tablespoons honey
• 1/4 teaspoon vanilla extract
• 1/4 cup walnuts, chopped

Instructions:
1. In a small saucepan over medium heat, combine figs, honey, and vanilla extract.
2. Cook for 8-10 minutes, stirring occasionally, until figs are softened and the mixture has thickened.
3. Remove from heat and let cool.
4. Once cooled, chill the fig compote in the refrigerator for at least 30 minutes.
5. To serve, spoon Greek yogurt into bowls, top with chilled fig compote, and sprinkle with chopped walnuts.

Nutrition Facts: Calories: 150 | Total Fat: 5g | Cholesterol: 5mg | Sodium: 20mg | Carbohydrates: 21g

Mediterranean Hummus Toast

Prep Time: 5 minutes | Cook Time: 5 minutes | Serves: 4

Ingredients:
• 4 slices whole grain bread, toasted
• 1 cup hummus
• 1 cup cherry tomatoes, halved
• 1/2 cucumber, thinly sliced
• 1/4 red onion, thinly sliced
• 1/4 cup Kalamata olives, pitted and chopped
• 2 tablespoons feta cheese, crumbled
• Fresh parsley for garnish
• Olive oil for drizzling
• Salt and pepper to taste

Instructions:
1. Spread a generous layer of hummus on each slice of toast.
2. Top with cherry tomatoes, cucumber slices, red onion, olives, and feta cheese.
3. Drizzle with olive oil, and season with salt and pepper.
4. Garnish with fresh parsley.
5. Serve immediately and enjoy!

Nutrition Facts: Calories: 250 | Total Fat: 13g | Cholesterol: 5mg | Sodium: 600mg | Carbohydrates: 26g

Baked Olives with Citrus and Herbs

Prep Time: 10 minutes | Cook Time: 15 minutes | Serves: 4

Ingredients:
• 2 cups mixed olives
• Zest of 1 lemon
• Zest of 1 orange
• 3 cloves garlic, minced
• 2 sprigs fresh rosemary
• 2 sprigs fresh thyme
• 1/4 cup olive oil
• Freshly ground black pepper to taste

Instructions:
1. Preheat your oven to 350°F (175°C).
2. In a mixing bowl, combine the olives, lemon zest, orange zest, garlic, rosemary, thyme, and olive oil.
3. Mix until the olives are well coated with the herbs and zest.
4. Transfer the olives to a baking dish and spread them out evenly.
5. Bake in the preheated oven for 15 minutes, stirring once halfway through.
6. Remove from the oven and let cool for a few minutes before serving.
7. Finish with freshly ground black pepper and serve warm.

Nutrition Facts: Calories: 200 | Total Fat: 20g | Sodium: 800mg | Total Carbohydrates: 5g

Stuffed Pita Pockets with Greek Salad

Prep Time: 15 minutes | Serves: 4

Ingredients:
• 4 whole wheat pita breads
• 1 cup cherry tomatoes, halved
• 1 cucumber, diced
• 1/4 red onion, thinly sliced
• 1/4 cup Kalamata olives, pitted and chopped
• 1/2 cup feta cheese, crumbled
• 2 tablespoons olive oil
• Juice of 1 lemon
• 1 teaspoon dried oregano
• Salt and pepper to taste

Instructions:
1. In a large bowl, combine the tomatoes, cucumber, red onion, olives, and feta cheese.
2. In a small bowl, whisk together the olive oil, lemon juice, oregano, salt, and pepper.
3. Pour the dressing over the salad and toss to combine.
4. Cut the pita breads in half to create pockets.
5. Stuff each pita pocket with the Greek salad mixture.
6. Serve immediately or wrap in foil for a portable meal.

Nutrition Facts: Calories: 300 | Total Fat: 15g | Cholesterol: 20mg | Sodium: 600mg | Carbohydrates: 35g

Marinated Feta Cheese with Herbs

Prep Time: 10 minutes (plus marinating time) | Serves: 4

Ingredients:
- 8 ounces feta cheese, cut into cubes
- 1/4 cup olive oil
- 2 cloves garlic, minced
- 1 teaspoon dried oregano
- 1 teaspoon dried thyme
- 1/2 teaspoon red pepper flakes (optional)
- Zest of 1 lemon
- Freshly ground black pepper to taste

Instructions:
1. Place the feta cheese cubes in a jar or bowl.
2. In a small bowl, combine the olive oil, garlic, oregano, thyme, red pepper flakes (if using), and lemon zest.
3. Pour the olive oil mixture over the feta cheese.
4. Ensure that the cheese is fully submerged in the marinade. If not, add more olive oil until it is.
5. Cover and refrigerate for at least 4 hours, or overnight for best results.
6. To serve, remove from the refrigerator and let come to room temperature.
7. Sprinkle with freshly ground black pepper and serve with crusty bread or crackers.

Nutrition Facts: Calories: 250 | Total Fat: 23g | Cholesterol: 50mg | Sodium: 700mg | Carbohydrates: 3g

Roasted Eggplant Dip with Pomegranate

Prep Time: 15 minutes | Cook Time: 25 minutes | Serves: 4

Ingredients:
- 1 large eggplant
- 2 tablespoons olive oil
- 2 cloves garlic, minced
- Juice of 1 lemon
- 1/4 cup tahini
- 1/4 cup pomegranate seeds
- 2 tablespoons fresh parsley, chopped
- Salt and pepper to taste

Instructions:
1. Preheat your oven to 400°F (200°C).
2. Cut the eggplant in half lengthwise and score the flesh in a diamond pattern.
3. Drizzle the olive oil over the cut sides of the eggplant and sprinkle with garlic.
4. Place the eggplant halves cut-side down on a baking sheet and roast for 25 minutes, or until the flesh is tender.
5. Remove from the oven and let cool for a few minutes.
6. Scoop out the flesh of the eggplant and place it in a food processor.
7. Add the lemon juice, tahini, salt, and pepper.
8. Pulse until smooth.
9. Transfer the dip to a serving bowl and garnish with pomegranate seeds and chopped parsley.
10. Serve with pita chips or fresh vegetables.

Nutrition Facts: Calories: 150 | Total Fat: 10g | Sodium: 15mg | Carbohydrates: 15g | Fiber: 5g

Chapter 7: Beverages

Greek Mountain Tea with Honey

Prep Time: 2 minutes | Serves: 1

Ingredients:
- 1 tablespoon dried Greek mountain tea (or 1 tea bag)
- 1 cup boiling water
- 1-2 teaspoons honey (or to taste)
- Lemon slice (optional)

Instructions:
1. Place the Greek mountain tea in a teapot or infuser.
2. Pour the boiling water over the tea leaves.
3. Cover and steep for 5-10 minutes, depending on desired strength.
4. Strain the tea into a cup.
5. Add honey to taste, stirring until it dissolves.
6. Add a slice of lemon if desired.
7. Serve hot and enjoy.

Nutrition Facts: Calories: 20 | Sodium: 2mg | Carbohydrates: 5.3g

Sparkling Mediterranean Citrus Punch

Prep Time: 10 minutes | Serves: 4-6

Ingredients:
- 1 cup fresh orange juice
- 1/2 cup fresh lemon juice
- 1/2 cup fresh lime juice
- 2 tablespoons sugar (adjust to taste)
- 2 cups sparkling water
- Ice cubes
- Orange, lemon, and lime slices for garnish
- Fresh mint leaves for garnish

Instructions:
1. In a pitcher, combine the fresh orange, lemon, and lime juices.
2. Add sugar and stir until it is completely dissolved.
3. Just before serving, add the sparkling water and stir gently to combine.
4. Fill glasses with ice cubes and pour the punch over.
5. Garnish with slices of orange, lemon, lime, and a sprig of fresh mint.
6. Serve immediately and enjoy.

Nutrition Facts: Calories: 40 | Sodium: 5mg | Total Carbohydrates: 10g

Fresh Pomegranate and Mint Juice

Prep Time: 10 minutes | Serves: 2

Ingredients:
- Seeds from 1 large pomegranate
- 1 tablespoon fresh mint leaves
- 1-2 teaspoons sugar or honey (optional)
- 2 cups cold water
- Ice cubes

Instructions:
1. In a blender, combine the pomegranate seeds, mint leaves, and 1 cup of water.
2. Blend on high until well mixed.
3. Strain the mixture through a fine-mesh sieve or cheesecloth into a pitcher, pressing to extract as much juice as possible.
4. Add the remaining water and stir.
5. Taste and add sugar or honey if desired, stirring until dissolved.
6. Serve over ice cubes in glasses.
7. Garnish with additional mint leaves if desired.
8. Enjoy your refreshing drink.

Nutrition Facts: Calories: 70 | Total Fat: 0.3g | Sodium: 5mg | Carbohydrates: 17g

Iced Greek Coffee

Prep Time: 2 minutes | Serves: 1

Ingredients:
- 1 heaped teaspoon Greek coffee
- 1 cup cold water
- Ice cubes
- Sugar (optional)

Instructions:
1. In a small pot, combine the Greek coffee and water. Add sugar if desired.
2. Place the pot over medium heat and bring to a boil, stirring occasionally.
3. Once the coffee starts to froth, remove from heat and let it settle.
4. Pour the coffee over a cup filled with ice cubes, making sure to include some of the foam on top.
5. Serve immediately and enjoy.

Nutrition Facts: Calories: 5 | Sodium: 1mg | Total Carbohydrates: 1g

Lavender and Lemon Infused Water

Prep Time: 5 minutes | Serves: 4

Ingredients:
- 1 tablespoon dried lavender buds (culinary grade)
- 1 lemon, thinly sliced
- 1 quart (4 cups) cold water
- Ice cubes

Instructions:
1. In a pitcher, combine the lavender buds and lemon slices.
2. Add the cold water.
3. Cover and refrigerate for at least 1 hour, allowing the flavors to infuse.
4. Strain the water to remove the lavender buds and lemon slices.
5. Serve over ice cubes in glasses.
6. Enjoy your calming and refreshing drink.

Nutrition Facts: Calories: 0 | Total Fat: 0g | Cholesterol: 0mg | Carbohydrates: 0g

Turkish Rose Lemonade

Prep Time: 10 minutes | Serves: 4

Ingredients:
- 2 tablespoons dried rose petals (edible grade)
- 1/2 cup freshly squeezed lemon juice
- 1/3 cup honey or sugar (adjust to taste)
- 4 cups cold water
- Ice cubes
- Lemon slices and rose petals for garnish

Instructions:
1. In a pitcher, combine the dried rose petals and lemon juice.
2. Add the honey or sugar, and stir until fully dissolved.
3. Add the cold water and stir well.
4. Refrigerate for at least 30 minutes to allow the flavors to infuse.
5. Strain the lemonade to remove the rose petals.
6. Serve over ice cubes in glasses, garnished with lemon slices and a few rose petals.
7. Enjoy your fragrant and refreshing drink.

Nutrition Facts: Calories: 50 | Sodium: 1mg | Carbohydrates: 13g | Sugars: 12g

Mediterranean Herbal Tea Blend

Prep Time: 5 minutes | Serves: 2

Ingredients:
- 1 tablespoon dried lavender buds
- 1 tablespoon dried chamomile flowers
- 1 tablespoon dried mint leaves
- 2 cups boiling water
- Honey or lemon slices (optional)

Instructions:
1. In a teapot or tea infuser, combine the lavender, chamomile, and mint.
2. Pour the boiling water over the herbs.
3. Cover and steep for 5-7 minutes.
4. Strain the tea into cups.
5. Add honey or a lemon slice if desired.
6. Serve hot and enjoy the calming effects of this herbal blend.

Nutrition Facts: Calories: 2 | Sodium: 1mg | Carbohydrates: 0.4g

Sparkling Blood Orange and Pomegranate Spritzer

Prep Time: 10 minutes | Serves: 4

Ingredients:
- 1 cup blood orange juice
- 1 cup pomegranate juice
- 2 cups sparkling water
- Ice cubes
- Blood orange slices and pomegranate seeds for garnish

Instructions:
1. In a pitcher, combine the blood orange juice and pomegranate juice.
2. Add the sparkling water and stir gently to combine.
3. Fill glasses with ice cubes and pour the spritzer over.
4. Garnish with slices of blood orange and a sprinkle of pomegranate seeds.
5. Serve immediately and enjoy.

Nutrition Facts: Calories: 80 | Sodium: 10mg | Carbohydrates: 20g | Fiber: 0.2g

Greek Yogurt Smoothie with Fresh Berries

Prep Time: 5 minutes | Serves: 2

Ingredients:
- 1 cup Greek yogurt
- 1 cup mixed fresh berries (such as strawberries, blueberries, raspberries)
- 1 banana
- 1 cup almond milk or milk of choice
- 1 tablespoon honey or maple syrup (optional)
- Ice cubes

Instructions:
1. In a blender, combine the Greek yogurt, mixed berries, banana, and almond milk.
2. Add honey or maple syrup if using.
3. Add ice cubes to achieve your desired consistency.
4. Blend until smooth.
5. Pour into glasses and serve immediately.
6. Enjoy your protein-packed, fruity drink.

Nutrition Facts: Calories: 150 | Total Fat: 2g | Cholesterol: 5mg | Sodium: 60mg | Carbohydrates: 28g

Mediterranean Iced Tea with Pomegranate and Mint

Prep Time: 10 minutes | Serves: 4

Ingredients:
- 4 tea bags of Mediterranean blend tea (or any herbal tea of your choice)
- 4 cups boiling water
- 1/2 cup pomegranate juice
- Fresh mint leaves
- Honey or sugar to taste (optional)
- Ice cubes

Instructions:
1. Place the tea bags in a large pitcher.
2. Pour the boiling water over the tea bags.
3. Let steep for 5-7 minutes, then remove the tea bags.
4. Allow the tea to cool to room temperature, then refrigerate until chilled.
5. Once chilled, add the pomegranate juice and mint leaves.
6. Add honey or sugar to taste if desired, stir well.
8. Serve over ice in glasses, garnished with additional mint leaves if desired.

Nutrition Facts: Calories: 30 | Sodium: 10mg | Carbohydrates: 7g

Lemon and Olive Leaf Tea

Prep Time: 5 minutes | Serves: 2

Ingredients:
- 1 tablespoon dried olive leaves
- 1 lemon, juiced
- 2 cups boiling water
- Honey or sweetener of choice, to taste

Instructions:
1. Place the olive leaves in a tea infuser or teapot.
2. Add the boiling water.
3. Let it steep for 5-7 minutes, depending on how strong you prefer your tea.
4. Add the fresh lemon juice.
5. Sweeten with honey or your choice of sweetener, if desired.
6. Strain the tea into cups.
7. Serve hot and enjoy the unique flavor and health benefits of olive leaf tea.

Nutrition Facts: Calories: 18 | Sodium: 1mg | Carbohydrates: 5g

Fresh Fig and Almond Milkshake

Prep Time: 5 minutes | Serves: 2

Ingredients:
- 6 fresh figs, stemmed and halved
- 2 cups almond milk
- 1 tablespoon honey or maple syrup
- A pinch of ground cinnamon
- Ice cubes

Instructions:
1. Place the figs, almond milk, honey (or maple syrup), and ground cinnamon in a blender.
2. Add a handful of ice cubes.
3. Blend on high until smooth.
4. Pour into glasses and serve immediately.
5. Enjoy your naturally sweet and nutty milkshake.

Nutrition Facts: Calories: 150 | Total Fat: 3g | Sodium: 180mg | Total Carbohydrates: 32g

Turkish Apple Tea

Prep Time: 5 minutes | Serves: 2

Ingredients:
- 2 tablespoons Turkish apple tea powder (or 2 bags of apple tea)
- 2 cups boiling water
- Apple slices and a cinnamon stick for garnish (optional)

Instructions:
1. Place the apple tea powder or bags in a teapot.
2. Add the boiling water.
3. Stir well (if using powder) or let the bags steep for 3-5 minutes.
4. Serve hot, garnished with apple slices and a cinnamon stick if desired.

5. Enjoy your sweet and aromatic Turkish delight.

Nutrition Facts: Calories: 15 | Sodium: 5mg | Carbohydrates: 4g

Mediterranean Detox Water with Cucumber and Lemon

Prep Time: 5 minutes | Serves: 4

Ingredients:
- 1 cucumber, thinly sliced
- 1 lemon, thinly sliced
- 1 quart (4 cups) cold water
- Ice cubes
- Fresh mint leaves for garnish (optional)

Instructions:
1. In a pitcher, combine the cucumber slices and lemon slices.
2. Add the cold water.
3. Let it chill in the refrigerator for at least 1 hour, allowing the flavors to infuse.
4. Serve over ice cubes in glasses, garnished with fresh mint leaves if using.
5. Enjoy your refreshing and detoxifying drink.

Nutrition Facts: Calories: 5 | Sodium: 1mg | Carbohydrates: 1g

Fresh Basil and Strawberry Lemonade

Prep Time: 10 minutes | Serves: 4

Ingredients:
- 1 cup fresh strawberries, hulled and halved
- 1 handful fresh basil leaves
- 1/2 cup freshly squeezed lemon juice
- 1/3 cup honey or sugar (adjust to taste)
- 4 cups cold water
- Ice cubes
- Strawberry slices and basil leaves for garnish

Instructions:
1. In a pitcher, muddle the strawberries and basil leaves together.
2. Add the fresh lemon juice and honey or sugar.
3. Add the cold water and stir well.
4. Refrigerate for at least 30 minutes to allow the flavors to infuse.
5. Serve over ice cubes in glasses, garnished with strawberry slices and basil leaves.
6. Enjoy your sweet, tangy, and refreshing drink.

Nutrition Facts: Calories: 70 | Sodium: 5mg | Carbohydrates: 19g | Fiber: 1g

Greek Frappe Coffee

Prep Time: 5 minutes | Serves: 1

Ingredients:
- 1 1/2 teaspoons instant coffee
- 1 teaspoon sugar (adjust to taste)
- Cold water
- Ice cubes
- A splash of milk (optional)

Instructions:
1. In a shaker or jar with a tight-fitting lid, combine the instant coffee, sugar, and a splash of cold water.
2. Shake vigorously for 30 seconds until the mixture becomes frothy.
3. Fill a glass halfway with ice cubes.
4. Pour the coffee mixture over the ice.
5. Top up with cold water, leaving a bit of space for milk if you're using it.
6. Add a splash of milk if desired.
7. Stir well before drinking.
8. Enjoy your refreshing and energizing Greek Frappe!

Nutrition Facts: Calories: 5 | Sodium: 2mg | Carbohydrates: 1g

Lavender Infused Honey Lemonade

Prep Time: 10 minutes (plus chilling time) | Serves: 4

Ingredients:
- 1/4 cup dried lavender buds
- 1/2 cup honey
- 3/4 cup fresh lemon juice
- 4 cups cold water
- Ice cubes
- Lemon slices and lavender sprigs for garnish

Instructions:
1. In a small saucepan, combine the lavender buds and honey with 1 cup of water.
2. Bring to a simmer, stirring until the honey is dissolved.
3. Remove from heat and let steep for 10 minutes.
4. Strain out the lavender buds and let the honey mixture cool.
5. In a pitcher, combine the lavender-infused honey, lemon juice, and cold water.
6. Refrigerate until chilled.
7. Serve over ice cubes in glasses, garnished with lemon slices and lavender sprigs.
8. Enjoy your fragrant and sweet lemonade!

Nutrition Facts: Calories: 140 | Sodium: 5mg | Carbohydrates: 37g

Pomegranate and Rose Water Spritzer

Prep Time: 5 minutes | Serves: 2

Ingredients:
- 1 cup pomegranate juice
- 1/2 teaspoon rose water (adjust to taste)
- 1 cup sparkling water
- Ice cubes
- Pomegranate seeds and rose petals for garnish (optional)

Instructions:
1. In a pitcher, combine the pomegranate juice and rose water.
2. Add the sparkling water and stir gently.
3. Fill glasses with ice cubes.
4. Pour the pomegranate mixture over the ice.
5. Garnish with pomegranate seeds and rose petals if using.
6. Serve immediately and enjoy your exotic spritzer!

Nutrition Facts: Calories: 75 | Sodium: 25mg | Carbohydrates: 18g

Fresh Mint and Lemon Iced Tea

Prep Time: 5 minutes (plus chilling time) | Serves: 4

Ingredients:
- A handful of fresh mint leaves
- 4 cups boiling water
- 3 tablespoons honey or sugar (adjust to taste)
- Juice of 2 lemons
- Ice cubes
- Lemon slices and mint sprigs for garnish

Instructions:
1. Place the mint leaves in a large pitcher.
2. Pour the boiling water over the mint and let steep for 5-10 minutes.
3. Remove the mint leaves and add the honey or sugar, stirring until dissolved.
4. Add the lemon juice and stir.
5. Refrigerate until chilled.
6. Serve over ice cubes in glasses, garnished with lemon slices and mint sprigs.
7. Enjoy your refreshing and minty iced tea!

Nutrition Facts: Calories: 40 | Sodium: 5mg | Carbohydrates: 11g

Turkish Pomegranate Tea

Prep Time: 5 minutes | Serves: 2

Ingredients:
- 2 bags of black tea or 2 tablespoons loose leaf black tea
- 1 cup boiling water
- 1/2 cup pomegranate juice
- Honey or sugar to taste
- Ice cubes
- Pomegranate seeds for garnish (optional)

Instructions:
1. Steep the tea bags or loose leaf tea in boiling water for 3-5 minutes, depending on how strong you like your tea.
2. Remove the tea bags or strain out the loose leaf tea.
3. Add the pomegranate juice and sweeten with honey or sugar to taste.
4. Let the tea mixture cool.
5. Serve over ice cubes in glasses, garnished with

pomegranate seeds if using.
6. Enjoy your refreshing and fruity Turkish Pomegranate Tea!

Nutrition Facts: Calories: 50 | Sodium: 5mg | Carbohydrates: 12g,

Mediterranean Sangria with Citrus and Pomegranate

Prep Time: 10 minutes (plus chilling time) | Serves: 6

Ingredients:
• 1 bottle of red wine (Spanish or Mediterranean preferred)
• 1/2 cup brandy
• 1/2 cup orange liqueur (such as Cointreau)
• 1/2 cup sugar (adjust to taste)
• 1 orange, thinly sliced
• 1 lemon, thinly sliced
• 1 lime, thinly sliced
• 1/2 cup pomegranate seeds
• 2 cups sparkling water or soda
• Ice cubes

Instructions:
1. In a large pitcher, combine the red wine, brandy, orange liqueur, and sugar. Stir until the sugar is dissolved.
2. Add the sliced citrus fruits and pomegranate seeds.
3. Refrigerate for at least 2 hours, allowing the flavors to meld.
4. Just before serving, add the sparkling water and stir gently.
5. Fill glasses with ice cubes and pour the sangria over the ice.
6. Garnish with additional fruit slices if desired.
7. Enjoy your festive and fruity Mediterranean Sangria!

Nutrition Facts: Calories: 250 | Sodium: 10mg | Carbohydrates: 29g | Fiber: 1g

Fresh Grape and Rosemary Juice

Prep Time: 5 minutes | Serves: 2

Ingredients:
• 2 cups fresh red grapes
• A sprig of fresh rosemary
• 1 cup cold water or crushed ice
• Honey or sugar to taste (optional)

Instructions:
1. In a blender, combine the grapes, rosemary, and water or crushed ice.
2. Blend on high speed until smooth.
3. Strain the mixture through a fine mesh sieve or cheesecloth to remove the pulp and rosemary leaves.
4. Sweeten with honey or sugar to taste if desired.
5. Serve chilled and enjoy your refreshing Fresh Grape and Rosemary Juice!

Nutrition Facts: Calories: 110 | Sodium: 3mg | Carbohydrates: 29g | Dietary Fiber: 1g

Greek Yogurt and Honey Smoothie

Prep Time: 5 minutes | Serves: 2

Ingredients:
• 1 cup Greek yogurt
• 2 tablespoons honey
• 1 banana
• 1/2 cup milk (dairy or plant-based)
• Ice cubes

Instructions:
1. In a blender, combine the Greek yogurt, honey, banana, and milk.
2. Add a handful of ice cubes.
3. Blend on high speed until smooth and creamy.
4. Pour into glasses and serve immediately.
5. Enjoy your creamy and sweet Greek Yogurt and Honey Smoothie!

Nutrition Facts: Calories: 180 | Total Fat: 2g | Cholesterol: 10mg | Sodium: 45mg | Carbohydrates: 33g | Dietary Fiber: 1g

Sparkling Fig and Elderflower Cocktail

Prep Time: 5 minutes | Serves: 2

Ingredients:
• 4 fresh figs (or dried figs, soaked in hot water)
• 2 ounces elderflower liqueur
• 1 bottle sparkling wine (chilled)
• Ice cubes

Instructions:
1. Muddle the figs in a cocktail shaker to release their juice.
2. Add the elderflower liqueur and a handful of ice cubes.
3. Shake well until the mixture is well-chilled.
4. Strain the mixture into champagne flutes or wine glasses.
5. Top with sparkling wine.
6. Stir gently and serve immediately.
7. Enjoy your elegant and unique Sparkling Fig and Elderflower Cocktail!

Nutrition Facts: Calories: 230 | Sodium: 10mg | Carbohydrates: 30g | Dietary Fiber: 2g

Mediterranean Herbal Infusion

Prep Time: 5 minutes | Serves: 2

Ingredients:
• 1 tablespoon dried lavender
• 1 tablespoon dried chamomile
• 1 tablespoon dried mint
• 2 cups boiling water
• Honey or sugar to taste (optional)

Instructions:
1. Place the dried lavender, chamomile, and mint in a tea infuser or directly in a teapot.

2. Pour the boiling water over the herbs.
3. Cover and let steep for 5-7 minutes, depending on your preferred strength.
4. Strain the infusion into cups, if you placed the herbs directly in the pot.
5. Sweeten with honey or sugar to taste if desired.
6. Serve hot and enjoy your soothing Mediterranean Herbal Infusion!

Nutrition Facts: Calories: 2 | Sodium: 2mg | Carbohydrates: 0.5g

Lemon and Sage Tonic

Prep Time: 5 minutes | Serves: 2

Ingredients:
• Juice of 2 lemons
• 6 fresh sage leaves
• 1 tablespoon honey (optional)
• 2 cups cold water or soda water
• Ice cubes

Instructions:
1. In a pitcher, muddle the sage leaves to release their flavor.
2. Add the lemon juice and honey (if using). Stir until well combined.
3. Pour in the cold water or soda water.
4. Fill glasses with ice cubes and pour the tonic over.
5. Stir gently and serve immediately.
6. Enjoy your refreshing Lemon and Sage Tonic!

Nutrition Facts: Calories: 30 | Sodium: 2mg | Carbohydrates: 9g

Lavender and Berry Iced Tea

Prep Time: 5 minutes | Serves: 4

Ingredients:
• 1 tablespoon dried lavender buds
• 1 cup mixed berries (fresh or frozen)
• 4 cups boiling water
• Honey or sugar to taste (optional)

Instructions:
1. Place the lavender buds and mixed berries in a large heatproof bowl.
2. Pour the boiling water over the top.
3. Let it steep for 10 minutes.
4. Strain the mixture through a fine-mesh sieve into a pitcher, pressing on the berries to extract all the juices.
5. Sweeten with honey or sugar to taste if desired.
6. Chill in the refrigerator for at least 2 hours.
7. Serve over ice and enjoy your fragrant Lavender and Berry Iced Tea!

Nutrition Facts: Calories: 15 | Sodium: 2mg | Carbohydrates: 4g | Dietary Fiber: 1g

Turkish Lemonade with Orange Blossom

Prep Time: 10 minutes | Serves: 4

Ingredients:
• Juice of 4 lemons
• 1 tablespoon orange blossom water
• 1/4 cup sugar (adjust to taste)
• 4 cups cold water
• Ice cubes

Instructions:
1. In a pitcher, combine the lemon juice, orange blossom water, and sugar.
2. Stir until the sugar is completely dissolved.
3. Add the cold water and stir again.
4. Taste and adjust sweetness if necessary.
5. Fill glasses with ice cubes and pour the lemonade over.
6. Serve immediately and enjoy your exotic Turkish Lemonade with Orange Blossom!

Nutrition Facts: Calories: 60 | Sodium: 1mg | Carbohydrates: 16g

Fresh Peach and Thyme Iced Tea

Prep Time: 10 minutes (plus chilling time) | Serves: 4

Ingredients:
• 4 fresh peaches, pitted and sliced
• 4 sprigs fresh thyme
• 4 tea bags (black or green tea)
• 4 cups boiling water
• Honey or sugar to taste (optional)

Instructions:
1. Place the peach slices and thyme sprigs in a large heatproof pitcher.
2. Add the tea bags.
3. Pour the boiling water over the top.
4. Let it steep for 5 minutes, then remove the tea bags.
5. Allow the mixture to cool to room temperature, then refrigerate until chilled.
6. Sweeten with honey or sugar to taste if desired.
7. Serve over ice and enjoy your aromatic Fresh Peach and Thyme Iced Tea!

Nutrition Facts: Calories: 60 | otal Fat: 0.2g | Sodium: 1mg | Carbohydrates: 15g | Dietary Fiber: 2g

Mediterranean Cooler with Lemon and Mint

Prep Time: 5 minutes | Serves: 2

Ingredients:
• Juice of 2 lemons
• 10 fresh mint leaves
• 2 teaspoons sugar (adjust to taste)
• 2 cups cold water or soda water
• Ice cubes

Instructions:

1. In a pitcher, muddle the mint leaves with the sugar to release their flavor.
2. Add the lemon juice and stir until the sugar is dissolved.
3. Pour in the cold water or soda water.
4. Fill glasses with ice cubes and pour the cooler over.
5. Stir gently and serve immediately.
6. Enjoy your refreshing Mediterranean Cooler with Lemon and Mint!

Nutrition Facts: Calories: 30 | Sodium: 2mg | Carbohydrates: 9g

Pomegranate and Lemon Verbena Tea

Prep Time: 10 minutes | Serves: 4

Ingredients:
- 1 cup fresh pomegranate seeds
- A handful of fresh lemon verbena leaves
- 4 cups boiling water
- Honey or sugar to taste (optional)

Instructions:
1. In a teapot or large jar, combine the pomegranate seeds and lemon verbena leaves.
2. Pour the boiling water over the mixture.
3. Let it steep for 5-7 minutes.
4. Strain the mixture into a pitcher, pressing on the solids to extract all the flavors.
5. Sweeten with honey or sugar to taste if desired.
6. Let it cool to room temperature, then refrigerate until chilled.
7. Serve over ice and enjoy your refreshing Pomegranate and Lemon Verbena Tea!

Nutrition Facts: Calories: 35 | Sodium: 2mg | Carbohydrates: 9g | Dietary Fiber: 1g

Iced Turkish Coffee

Prep Time: 5 minutes | Serves: 1

Ingredients:
- 1 shot of Turkish coffee, brewed and chilled
- 1 cup cold milk or water
- Ice cubes
- Sugar to taste (optional)

Instructions:
1. Brew a shot of Turkish coffee and let it chill in the refrigerator.
2. Fill a glass with ice cubes.
3. Pour the chilled Turkish coffee over the ice.
4. Add cold milk or water.
5. Sweeten with sugar to taste if desired.
6. Stir well and enjoy your unique Iced Turkish Coffee!

Nutrition Facts: Calories: 30 | Total Fat: 1g | Cholesterol: 5mg | Sodium: 50mg | Total Carbohydrates: 3g

Sparkling Rose and Pomegranate Cocktail

Prep Time: 5 minutes | Serves: 1

Ingredients:
- 1/2 cup pomegranate juice
- 1/2 cup sparkling rosé wine
- Pomegranate seeds for garnish
- Ice cubes

Instructions:
1. In a champagne flute or wine glass, combine the pomegranate juice and sparkling rosé wine.
2. Add ice cubes.
3. Garnish with pomegranate seeds.
4. Stir gently and serve immediately.
5. Enjoy your festive Sparkling Rose and Pomegranate Cocktail!

Nutrition Facts: Calories: 120 | Sodium: 10mg | Carbohydrates: 15g

Fresh Apricot and Lavender Lemonade

Prep Time: 10 minutes (plus chilling time) | Serves: 4

Ingredients:
- 6 fresh apricots, pitted and sliced
- 1 tablespoon dried lavender buds
- Juice of 3 lemons
- 4 cups cold water
- Honey or sugar to taste (optional)

Instructions:
1. In a blender, combine the apricot slices, lavender buds, and lemon juice.
2. Blend until smooth.
3. Strain the mixture through a fine-mesh sieve into a pitcher.
4. Add the cold water and stir well.
5. Sweeten with honey or sugar to taste if desired.
6. Chill in the refrigerator for at least 2 hours.
7. Serve over ice and enjoy your fragrant Fresh Apricot and Lavender Lemonade!

Nutrition Facts: Calories: 50 | Sodium: 2mg | Carbohydrates: 13g | Dietary Fiber: 2g

Greek Yogurt and Mango Lassi

Prep Time: 5 minutes | Serves: 2

Ingredients:
- 1 cup Greek yogurt
- 1 mango, peeled and chopped
- 1/2 cup milk or water
- Honey or sugar to taste (optional)
- Ice cubes
- A pinch of ground cardamom (optional)

Instructions:
1. In a blender, combine the Greek yogurt, mango, milk or water, and ice cubes.

2. Blend until smooth.
3. Sweeten with honey or sugar to taste if desired.
4. Add a pinch of ground cardamom if using.
5. Pour into glasses and serve immediately.
6. Enjoy your creamy and tropical Greek Yogurt and Mango Lassi!

Nutrition Facts: Calories: 150 | Total Fat: 2g | Cholesterol: 10mg | Sodium: 60mg | Carbohydrates: 27g

Fresh Orange and Rosemary Juice

Prep Time: 5 minutes | Serves: 2

Ingredients:
• 4 large oranges, juiced
• 1 sprig of fresh rosemary
• Ice cubes (optional)

Instructions:
1. In a pitcher, combine fresh orange juice and rosemary sprig.
2. Let it infuse for about 5 minutes.
3. Remove the rosemary and serve the juice over ice cubes if desired.
4. Enjoy your aromatic and refreshing Fresh Orange and Rosemary Juice!

Nutrition Facts: Calories: 112 | Total Fat: 0.3g | Sodium: 2mg | Carbohydrates: 27g

Sparkling Mediterranean Berry Punch

Prep Time: 10 minutes | Serves: 4

Ingredients:
• 2 cups mixed berries (strawberries, raspberries, blueberries)
• 1 liter sparkling water
• Juice of 2 lemons
• Fresh mint leaves for garnish
• Ice cubes

Instructions:
1. In a large pitcher, muddle the berries to release their juices.
2. Add the lemon juice and sparkling water.
3. Stir gently to combine.
4. Serve over ice and garnish with fresh mint leaves.
5. Enjoy your fizzy and fruity Sparkling Mediterranean Berry Punch!

Nutrition Facts: Calories: 50 | Total Fat: 0.2g | Sodium: 4mg | Carbohydrates: 13g | Dietary Fiber: 3g,

Lemon and Thyme Infused Water

Prep Time: 5 minutes | Serves: 4

Ingredients:
• 1 lemon, thinly sliced
• A few sprigs of fresh thyme
• 1 quart (4 cups) cold water
• Ice cubes

Instructions:
1. In a pitcher, combine the lemon slices and thyme sprigs.
2. Add the cold water.
3. Let it infuse in the refrigerator for at least 1 hour.
4. Serve over ice cubes in glasses.
5. Enjoy your refreshing Lemon and Thyme Infused Water!

Nutrition Facts: Calories: 2 | Carbohydrates: 1g

Fresh Fig and Pomegranate Juice

Prep Time: 10 minutes | Serves: 2

Ingredients:
• 6 fresh figs, stems removed
• 1 cup fresh pomegranate seeds
• 2 cups cold water
• Honey or sugar to taste (optional)

Instructions:
1. In a blender, combine the figs, pomegranate seeds, and water.
2. Blend until smooth.
3. Strain the mixture through a fine-mesh sieve into a pitcher.
4. Sweeten with honey or sugar to taste if desired.
5. Serve over ice if desired.
6. Enjoy your sweet and tangy Fresh Fig and Pomegranate Juice!

Nutrition Facts: Calories: 120 | Total Fat: 0.3g | Sodium: 3mg | Carbohydrates: 31g | Dietary Fiber: 5g,

Turkish Delight Smoothie

Prep Time: 5 minutes | Serves: 1

Ingredients:
• 1 cup milk (dairy or plant-based)
• 1 banana
• 1 tablespoon rose water
• 1 teaspoon honey or sugar (optional)
• A pinch of ground cardamom
• Ice cubes

Instructions:
1. In a blender, combine all the ingredients with a handful of ice cubes.
2. Blend until smooth.
3. Taste and adjust sweetness if necessary.
4. Pour into a glass and enjoy your exotic Turkish Delight Smoothie!

Nutrition Facts: Calories: 180 | Total Fat: 3g | Cholesterol: 10mg | Sodium: 100mg | Carbohydrates: 34g

Greek Mountain Iced Tea

Prep Time: 5 minutes | Cook Time: 5 minutes | Serves: 2

Ingredients:
• 1 tablespoon Greek mountain tea leaves

- 2 cups boiling water
- Ice cubes
- Lemon slices and honey (optional), for serving

Instructions:
1. Place the Greek mountain tea leaves in a teapot or heatproof pitcher.
2. Pour the boiling water over the tea leaves.
3. Let steep for 5 minutes, then strain to remove the leaves.
4. Allow the tea to cool to room temperature, then refrigerate until chilled.
5. Serve over ice with lemon slices and honey if desired.
6. Enjoy your refreshing Greek Mountain Iced Tea!

Nutrition Facts: Calories: 2 | Carbohydrates: 0.5g

Fresh Berry and Basil Lemonade

Prep Time: 10 minutes | Serves: 4

Ingredients:
- 1 cup fresh berries (strawberries, blueberries, raspberries)
- 1 handful fresh basil leaves
- 1/2 cup lemon juice
- 1/4 cup honey or sugar (adjust to taste)
- 4 cups cold water
- Ice cubes

Instructions:
1. In a pitcher, muddle the fresh berries and basil leaves together.
2. Add the lemon juice and honey or sugar, and stir until well mixed.
3. Pour in the cold water and stir again.
4. Serve over ice in glasses.
5. Enjoy your fragrant and fruity Fresh Berry and Basil Lemonade!

Nutrition Facts: Calories: 50 | Total Fat: 0.2g | Sodium: 5mg | Carbohydrates: 13g | Dietary Fiber: 1g

Mediterranean Green Tea with Mint

Prep Time: 5 minutes | Cook Time: 3 minutes | Serves: 2

Ingredients:
- 2 green tea bags or 2 teaspoons loose green tea leaves
- A handful of fresh mint leaves
- 2 cups boiling water
- Honey or sugar to taste (optional)
- Ice cubes

Instructions:
1. Place the tea bags or loose tea leaves and fresh mint leaves in a teapot or heatproof pitcher.
2. Pour the boiling water over the tea and mint.
3. Let steep for 3 minutes, then strain to remove the tea leaves and mint.
4. Allow the tea to cool to room temperature, then refrigerate until chilled.
5. Serve over ice with honey or sugar if desired.
6. Enjoy your aromatic Mediterranean Green Tea with

Mint!

Nutrition Facts: Calories: 2 | Sodium: 1mg | Carbohydrates: 0.5g

Sparkling Citrus and Pomegranate Mimosa

Prep Time: 5 minutes | Serves: 4

Ingredients:
- 1 cup pomegranate juice, chilled
- 1 cup sparkling water or champagne, chilled
- 1 orange, juiced
- Pomegranate seeds and orange slices for garnish

Instructions:
1. In a pitcher, combine the pomegranate juice, sparkling water or champagne, and orange juice.
2. Stir gently to mix.
3. Pour into champagne flutes or glasses, and garnish with pomegranate seeds and orange slices.
4. Cheers and enjoy your celebratory Sparkling Citrus and Pomegranate Mimosa!

Nutrition Facts: Calories: 60 | Total Fat: 0.1g | Sodium: 12mg | Carbohydrates: 15g

Fresh Cherry and Almond Smoothie

Prep Time: 5 minutes | Serves: 2

Ingredients:
- 1 cup fresh cherries, pitted
- 1 cup almond milk
- 1 banana
- A drop of almond extract (optional)
- Ice cubes

Instructions:
1. In a blender, combine the cherries, almond milk, banana, and almond extract if using.
2. Add a handful of ice cubes.
3. Blend until smooth.
4. Pour into glasses and serve immediately.
5. Enjoy your luscious Fresh Cherry and Almond Smoothie!

Nutrition Facts: Calories: 130 | Total Fat: 1.5g | Sodium: 90mg | Carbohydrates: 29g

Turkish Citrus and Pomegranate Tea

Prep Time: 5 minutes | Cook Time: 5 minutes | Serves: 4

Ingredients:
- 4 bags of black tea or 4 teaspoons of loose black tea leaves
- 1 lemon, juiced
- 1 orange, juiced
- 1 cup pomegranate juice
- 4 cups boiling water
- Honey or sugar to taste (optional)
- Lemon slices and pomegranate seeds for garnish

Instructions:
1. Place the tea bags or loose tea leaves in a teapot or heatproof pitcher.
2. Pour the boiling water over the tea.
3. Let steep for 5 minutes, then remove the tea bags or strain out the loose tea leaves.
4. Add the lemon juice, orange juice, and pomegranate juice to the tea.
5. Stir in honey or sugar to taste, if desired.
6. Allow the tea to cool to room temperature, then refrigerate until chilled.
7. Serve over ice, garnished with lemon slices and pomegranate seeds.
8. Enjoy your fragrant and fruity Turkish Citrus and Pomegranate Tea!

Nutrition Facts: Calories: 60 | Sodium: 10mg | Carbohydrates: 15g

Lemon and Lavender Iced Tea

Prep Time: 10 minutes | Cook Time: 5 minutes | Serves: 4

Ingredients:
- 4 black or green tea bags or 4 teaspoons of loose tea leaves
- 1 tablespoon dried lavender buds (culinary grade)
- 1 lemon, juiced
- 4 cups boiling water
- Honey or sugar to taste (optional)
- Lemon slices for garnish

Instructions:
1. Place the tea bags or loose tea leaves and lavender buds in a teapot or heatproof pitcher.
2. Pour the boiling water over the tea and lavender.
3. Let steep for 5 minutes, then strain to remove the tea leaves and lavender buds.
4. Stir in the lemon juice.
5. Add honey or sugar to taste, if desired.
6. Allow the tea to cool to room temperature, then refrigerate until chilled.
7. Serve over ice, garnished with lemon slices.
8. Enjoy your refreshing Lemon and Lavender Iced Tea!

Nutrition Facts: Calories: 15 | Sodium: 5mg | Carbohydrates: 4g

Fresh Grapefruit and Rosemary Juice

Prep Time: 10 minutes | Serves: 4

Ingredients:
- 4 large grapefruits, juiced
- A sprig of fresh rosemary
- Ice cubes
- Rosemary sprigs and grapefruit slices for garnish

Instructions:
1. In a pitcher, combine the fresh grapefruit juice and the sprig of rosemary.
2. Allow the rosemary to infuse the juice for at least 30 minutes.
3. Remove the rosemary sprig and stir the juice well.

4. Serve over ice, garnished with rosemary sprigs and grapefruit slices.
5. Enjoy your aromatic and tangy Fresh Grapefruit and Rosemary Juice!

Nutrition Facts: Calories: 90 | Carbohydrates: 22g

Mediterranean Citrus and Honey Elixir

Prep Time: 5 minutes | Serves: 4

Ingredients:
- 1 orange, juiced
- 1 lemon, juiced
- 1 lime, juiced
- 1 tablespoon honey
- 4 cups cold water
- Ice cubes
- Citrus slices for garnish

Instructions:
1. In a pitcher, combine the orange juice, lemon juice, lime juice, and honey.
2. Stir well until the honey is fully dissolved.
3. Add the cold water and stir again.
4. Serve over ice, garnished with citrus slices.
5. Enjoy your sweet and zesty Mediterranean Citrus and Honey Elixir!

Nutrition Facts: Calories: 40 | Carbohydrates: 10g

Sparkling Peach and Thyme Lemonade

Prep Time: 10 minutes | Serves: 4

Ingredients:
- 2 peaches, pitted and sliced
- 1 lemon, juiced
- 4 sprigs of fresh thyme
- 1 tablespoon honey or sugar (optional)
- 4 cups sparkling water
- Ice cubes
- Peach slices and thyme sprigs for garnish

Instructions:
1. In a pitcher, muddle the peach slices and thyme sprigs to release their flavors.
2. Add the lemon juice and honey or sugar, if using, and stir well.
3. Add the sparkling water and stir again.
4. Serve over ice, garnished with peach slices and thyme sprigs.
5. Enjoy your fruity and herby Sparkling Peach and Thyme Lemonade!

Nutrition Facts: Calories: 40 | Sodium: 10mg | Carbohydrates: 10g | Dietary Fiber: 1g

Chapter 8: Desserts

Greek Yogurt with Honey and Walnuts

Prep Time: 5 minutes | Serves: 4

Ingredients:
- 4 cups Greek yogurt
- 1/2 cup honey
- 1 cup walnuts, chopped
- A pinch of cinnamon (optional)

Instructions:
1. Divide the Greek yogurt evenly between four bowls or serving glasses.
2. Drizzle each serving with honey.
3. Sprinkle chopped walnuts on top.
4. Add a pinch of cinnamon if desired.
5. Serve immediately and enjoy your creamy and crunchy Greek Yogurt with Honey and Walnuts!

Nutrition Facts: Calories: 350 | Total Fat: 20g | Cholesterol: 10mg | Sodium: 60mg | Carbohydrates: 26g

Lemon Olive Oil Cake

Prep Time: 15 minutes | Cook Time: 40 minutes | Serves: 8

Ingredients:
- 1 3/4 cups all-purpose flour
- 2 teaspoons baking powder
- 1/2 teaspoon salt
- 1 cup sugar
- 3 large eggs
- 1 cup extra-virgin olive oil
- 3/4 cup milk
- Zest and juice of 1 lemon

Instructions:
1. Preheat your oven to 350°F (175°C). Grease and flour a 9-inch round cake pan.
2. In a medium bowl, whisk together the flour, baking powder, and salt.
3. In a large bowl, beat together the sugar and eggs until light and fluffy.
4. Gradually add the olive oil, beating continuously.
5. Add the flour mixture in three additions, alternating with the milk, beginning and ending with the flour.
6. Stir in the lemon zest and juice.
7. Pour the batter into the prepared pan.
8. Bake for 40-45 minutes, or until a toothpick inserted into the center comes out clean.
9. Allow the cake to cool in the pan for 10 minutes, then transfer to a wire rack to cool completely.
10. Slice and serve your moist and flavorful Lemon Olive Oil Cake!

Nutrition Facts: Calories: 460 | Total Fat: 27g | Cholesterol: 70mg | Sodium: 230mg | Carbohydrates: 49g

Pistachio Baklava

Prep Time: 30 minutes | Cook Time: 1 hour | Serves: 12

Ingredients:
- 2 cups pistachios, finely chopped
- 1/4 cup sugar
- 1 teaspoon ground cinnamon
- 1 cup melted butter
- 1 package phyllo dough, thawed
- 1 cup honey
- 1/2 cup water
- 1/2 cup sugar
- 1 teaspoon vanilla extract

Instructions:
1. Preheat your oven to 350°F (175°C).
2. In a bowl, combine the chopped pistachios, 1/4 cup sugar, and ground cinnamon.
3. Brush a 9x13-inch baking dish with melted butter.
4. Place one sheet of phyllo dough in the dish, and brush with more melted butter. Repeat with 7 more sheets, brushing each with butter.
5. Sprinkle a thin layer of the pistachio mixture over the phyllo.
6. Continue layering and buttering the phyllo sheets, sprinkling every second sheet with the pistachio mixture, until all the pistachios are used.
7. Finish with a final layer of 8 buttered phyllo sheets.
8. Using a sharp knife, cut the baklava into diamonds or squares.
9. Bake for 50-60 minutes, or until golden and crisp.
10. While the baklava is baking, combine the honey, 1/2 cup water, 1/2 cup sugar, and vanilla in a saucepan. Bring to a simmer, stirring until the sugar is dissolved. Simmer for 10 minutes.
11. Remove the baklava from the oven and immediately pour the honey syrup over it.
12. Allow the baklava to cool completely in the pan before serving.
13. Enjoy your sweet and nutty Pistachio Baklava!

Nutrition Facts: Calories: 420 | Total Fat: 22g | Cholesterol: 30mg | Sodium: 190mg | Carbohydrates: 52g

Fig and Almond Tart

Prep Time: 20 minutes | Cook Time: 35 minutes | Serves: 8

Ingredients:
- 1 1/4 cups all-purpose flour
- 1/4 cup sugar
- 1/2 teaspoon salt
- 1/2 cup unsalted butter, cold and cubed
- 1 large egg yolk
- 2 tablespoons ice water
- 3/4 cup almond meal or ground almonds
- 1/4 cup sugar
- 1/2 cup unsalted butter, softened
- 1 large egg
- 1 teaspoon vanilla extract
- 8-10 fresh figs, halved

• Honey for drizzling (optional)

Instructions:
1. In a food processor, combine flour, 1/4 cup sugar, and salt. Add the cold butter and pulse until the mixture resembles coarse crumbs.
2. Mix the egg yolk with ice water, and add to the food processor. Pulse until the dough just comes together.
3. Turn the dough out onto a piece of plastic wrap, shape into a disk, wrap, and chill for at least 30 minutes.
4. Preheat your oven to 375°F (190°C).
5. On a lightly floured surface, roll out the dough to fit a 9-inch tart pan. Press the dough into the pan and trim any excess.
6. In a bowl, beat together 1/4 cup sugar, 1/2 cup butter, egg, and vanilla until smooth. Stir in the almond meal.
7. Spread the almond mixture over the tart crust.
8. Arrange the fig halves, cut side up, over the almond mixture.
9. Bake for 35-40 minutes, or until the almond filling is set and the crust is golden.
10. Drizzle with honey if desired.
11. Allow the tart to cool before serving.
12. Slice and enjoy your fruity and nutty Fig and Almond Tart!

Nutrition Facts: Calories: 410 | otal Fat: 27g | Cholesterol: 90mg | Sodium: 160mg | Carbohydrates: 38g

Turkish Delight

Prep Time: 10 minutes | Cook Time: 1 hour | Serves: 16

Ingredients:
• 4 cups sugar
• 4 1/2 cups water, divided
• 2 teaspoons lemon juice
• 1 cup cornstarch
• 1 teaspoon cream of tartar
• 1 1/2 teaspoons rose water
• Pink food coloring (optional)
• Powdered sugar for dusting

Instructions:
1. In a large saucepan, combine the sugar, 1 1/2 cups water, and lemon juice. Bring to a boil, stirring until the sugar is dissolved. Simmer for 15 minutes without stirring.
2. In a separate bowl, mix the cornstarch, cream of tartar, and remaining 3 cups water until smooth.
3. Gradually add the cornstarch mixture to the sugar syrup, stirring constantly.
4. Bring the mixture to a boil, then reduce the heat and simmer for 45-60 minutes, stirring frequently, until the mixture becomes a thick, opaque paste.
5. Remove from heat and stir in the rose water and food coloring if using.
6. Pour the mixture into a greased 9x9-inch pan, smoothing the top with a spatula.
7. Allow to cool and set for several hours or overnight.
8. Cut into squares and dust with powdered sugar.
9. Enjoy your sweet and fragrant Turkish Delight!

Nutrition Facts: Calories: 280 | Sodium: 10mg | Carbohydrates: 70g

Mediterranean Poached Pears in Red Wine

Prep Time: 15 minutes | Cook Time: 1 hour | Serves: 4

Ingredients:
• 4 ripe pears, peeled and cored
• 1 bottle red wine
• 1 cup sugar
• 2 cinnamon sticks
• 4 cloves
• 1 orange, zest and juice
• 1 lemon, zest and juice

Instructions:
1. In a large saucepan, combine the red wine, sugar, cinnamon sticks, cloves, orange zest and juice, and lemon zest and juice.
2. Bring to a simmer over medium heat, stirring until the sugar is dissolved.
3. Add the pears to the saucepan, making sure they are fully submerged in the wine mixture.
4. Reduce the heat to low, cover, and simmer for 45-60 minutes, or until the pears are tender.
5. Carefully remove the pears from the liquid and set aside.
6. Increase the heat to medium-high and continue to cook the wine mixture for another 15-20 minutes, or until it has reduced by half and thickened slightly.
7. Strain the sauce through a fine-mesh sieve and discard the spices.
8. To serve, place each pear on a plate and drizzle with the red wine reduction.
9. Enjoy your elegant Mediterranean Poached Pears in Red Wine!

Nutrition Facts: Calories: 400 | Sodium: 10mg | Carbohydrates: 80g | Dietary Fiber: 5g

Orange Blossom Panna Cotta

Prep Time: 15 minutes | Cook Time: 5 minutes (plus 4 hours setting time) | Serves: 4

Ingredients:
• 2 cups heavy cream
• 1/4 cup sugar
• 1 vanilla bean, split and seeds scraped
• 2 teaspoons gelatin powder
• 2 tablespoons water
• 1 tablespoon orange blossom water

Instructions:
1. In a small bowl, sprinkle the gelatin over the water and let it sit for 5 minutes to bloom.
2. In a saucepan, combine the heavy cream, sugar, and vanilla bean seeds. Heat over medium heat until the sugar is dissolved and the mixture is hot, but not boiling.
3. Remove from the heat and stir in the bloomed gelatin until fully dissolved.
4. Add the orange blossom water and stir to combine.

5. Strain the mixture through a fine-mesh sieve into a jug or bowl.
6. Pour the mixture into 4 ramekins or molds.
7. Refrigerate for at least 4 hours, or until set.
8. To serve, run a knife around the edge of each panna cotta and unmold onto a plate.
9. Enjoy your fragrant Orange Blossom Panna Cotta!

Nutrition Facts: Calories: 470 | Total Fat: 44g | Cholesterol: 160mg | Sodium: 45mg | Carbohydrates: 18g

Baklava Cheesecake

Prep Time: 30 minutes | Cook Time: 1 hour 15 minutes | Serves: 12

Ingredients:
• 2 packages phyllo dough, thawed
• 1 cup unsalted butter, melted
• 2 cups walnuts, chopped
• 1/4 cup sugar
• 1 teaspoon ground cinnamon
• 3 packages cream cheese, softened
• 1 cup sugar
• 3 large eggs
• 1 teaspoon vanilla extract
• 1 cup Greek yogurt
• Honey for drizzling

Instructions:
1. Preheat your oven to 325°F (160°C). Grease a 9-inch springform pan.
2. In a bowl, combine the chopped walnuts, 1/4 cup sugar, and ground cinnamon. Set aside.
3. Place one sheet of phyllo dough on a clean surface and brush with melted butter. Layer another sheet on top and brush with more butter. Repeat until you have 5 layers.
4. Press the phyllo layers into the bottom of the prepared pan. Sprinkle with half of the walnut mixture.
5. In a large bowl, beat together the cream cheese and 1 cup sugar until smooth and creamy.
6. Add the eggs one at a time, beating well after each addition. Stir in the vanilla extract and Greek yogurt.
7. Pour half of the cream cheese mixture over the walnut layer in the pan.
8. Repeat the phyllo layering process with another 5 sheets and place on top of the cream cheese layer. Sprinkle with the remaining walnut mixture.
9. Pour the remaining cream cheese mixture on top.
10. Bake for 1 hour 15 minutes, or until the center is set and the top is golden brown.
11. Allow to cool in the pan for 10 minutes, then run a knife around the edge and remove the sides of the pan.
12. Drizzle with honey before serving, enjoy your decadent Baklava Cheesecake!

Nutrition Facts: Calories: 580 | Total Fat: 40g | Cholesterol: 150mg | Sodium: 350mg | Carbohydrates: 45g

Olive Oil and Lemon Biscotti

Prep Time: 20 minutes | Cook Time: 40 minutes | Serves: 24

Ingredients:
• 2 1/2 cups all-purpose flour
• 1 1/2 teaspoons baking powder
• 1/2 teaspoon salt
• 1 cup sugar
• 1/2 cup olive oil
• 2 large eggs
• Zest of 1 lemon
• 2 tablespoons fresh lemon juice
• 1/2 teaspoon vanilla extract

Instructions:
1. Preheat your oven to 350°F (175°C). Line a baking sheet with parchment paper.
2. In a bowl, whisk together the flour, baking powder, and salt. Set aside.
3. In another bowl, beat together the sugar, olive oil, eggs, lemon zest, lemon juice, and vanilla extract until well combined.
4. Gradually add the dry ingredients to the wet ingredients, mixing just until combined.
5. Divide the dough in half and shape each half into a log, about 12 inches long and 2 inches wide. Place the logs on the prepared baking sheet, spacing them apart.
6. Bake for 25 minutes, or until the logs are light golden brown.
7. Remove from the oven and allow to cool for 10 minutes.
8. Transfer the logs to a cutting board and slice diagonally into 1/2-inch thick slices.
9. Place the slices, cut side down, back on the baking sheet.
10. Bake for an additional 15 minutes, or until crisp and golden.
11. Cool on a wire rack, enjoy your Olive Oil and Lemon Biscotti with your favorite tea or coffee!

Nutrition Facts: Calories: 150 | Total Fat: 6g | Cholesterol: 15mg | Sodium: 65mg | Carbohydrates: 21g

Rose Water and Pistachio Ice Cream

Prep Time: 15 minutes | Cook Time: 10 minutes | Serves: 6

Ingredients:
• 2 cups heavy cream
• 1 cup whole milk
• 3/4 cup sugar
• 1/2 cup shelled pistachios, chopped
• 1 teaspoon rose water
• A pinch of salt

Instructions:
1. In a saucepan over medium heat, combine the heavy cream, milk, and sugar. Stir until the sugar is dissolved and the mixture is heated through.
2. Remove from heat and stir in the chopped pistachios, rose water, and salt.
3. Allow the mixture to cool to room temperature, then

cover and refrigerate until chilled.
4. Once chilled, pour the mixture into an ice cream maker and churn according to the manufacturer's instructions.
5. Transfer the churned ice cream to a container and freeze until firm.
6. Serve your Rose Water and Pistachio Ice Cream in bowls or cones.
7. Enjoy your luxurious and aromatic dessert!

Nutrition Facts: Calories: 360 | Total Fat: 26g | Cholesterol: 80mg | Sodium: 40mg | Carbohydrates: 30g

Greek Honey Puffs (Loukoumades)

Prep Time: 20 minutes | Cook Time: 15 minutes | Serves: 6

Ingredients:
- 2 cups all-purpose flour
- 1 tablespoon sugar
- 1 packet (2 1/4 teaspoons) active dry yeast
- 1/2 teaspoon salt
- 1 cup warm water (110°F or 45°C)
- Vegetable oil for frying
- 1 cup honey
- 1 teaspoon cinnamon
- Powdered cinnamon and chopped walnuts for garnish

Instructions:
1. In a large bowl, combine the flour, sugar, yeast, and salt.
2. Add the warm water and stir until the batter is smooth.
3. Cover the bowl with a cloth and let it rise in a warm place for about 1 hour, or until doubled in size.
4. In a deep frying pan or pot, heat the vegetable oil to 350°F (175°C).
5. Drop teaspoonfuls of the batter into the hot oil and fry until golden brown on all sides.
6. Remove the honey puffs with a slotted spoon and drain on paper towels.
7. In a separate saucepan, heat the honey until it is warm.
8. Dip the fried honey puffs in the warm honey, ensuring they are well coated.
9. Sprinkle with powdered cinnamon and chopped walnuts.
10. Serve warm and enjoy your Greek Honey Puffs!

Nutrition Facts: Calories: 390 | Total Fat: 15g | Sodium: 210mg | Carbohydrates: 61g

Lemon Lavender Sorbet

Prep Time: 10 minutes | Cook Time: 5 minutes | Serves: 4

Ingredients:
- 1 cup sugar
- 1 tablespoon dried lavender buds
- Zest of 1 lemon
- 1 cup fresh lemon juice
- 2 cups water

Instructions:
1. In a saucepan, combine the sugar, lavender buds,

lemon zest, and water.
2. Bring to a boil, stirring until the sugar is dissolved.
3. Remove from heat and let the mixture steep for 5 minutes.
4. Strain the mixture through a fine-mesh sieve, discarding the lavender and lemon zest.
5. Stir in the fresh lemon juice.
6. Chill the mixture in the refrigerator until cold.
7. Once chilled, pour the mixture into an ice cream maker and churn according to the manufacturer's instructions.
8. Transfer the sorbet to a container and freeze until firm.
9. Serve the Lemon Lavender Sorbet in bowls or glasses.
10. Enjoy your refreshing and aromatic dessert!

Nutrition Facts: Calories: 220 | Carbohydrates: 57g

Mediterranean Almond Cookies

Prep Time: 15 minutes | Cook Time: 15 minutes | Serves: 24

Ingredients:
- 2 cups ground almonds
- 1 cup powdered sugar
- 2 egg whites
- 1 teaspoon almond extract
- A pinch of salt
- Sliced almonds for garnish

Instructions:
1. Preheat your oven to 350°F (175°C) and line a baking sheet with parchment paper.
2. In a bowl, combine the ground almonds and powdered sugar.
3. In another bowl, beat the egg whites and salt until stiff peaks form.
4. Gently fold the almond mixture into the egg whites, adding the almond extract.
5. Drop teaspoonfuls of the batter onto the prepared baking sheet, spacing them apart.
6. Press a sliced almond into the top of each cookie.
7. Bake for 12-15 minutes, or until the edges are golden brown.
8. Allow the cookies to cool on the baking sheet for 5 minutes, then transfer to a wire rack to cool completely.
9. Enjoy your Mediterranean Almond Cookies!

Nutrition Facts: Calories: 70 | Total Fat: 4g | Sodium: 10mg | Carbohydrates: 7g

Pomegranate and Honey Tart

Prep Time: 25 minutes | Cook Time: 35 minutes | Serves: 8

Ingredients:
- 1 pre-made tart crust
- 1 cup pomegranate juice
- 1/4 cup honey
- 3 large eggs
- 1 teaspoon vanilla extract
- A pinch of salt
- Fresh pomegranate seeds for garnish

Instructions:
1. Preheat your oven to 350°F (175°C).
2. Place the tart crust in a tart pan and set aside.
3. In a saucepan, reduce the pomegranate juice over medium heat to about 1/4 cup. Let it cool.
4. In a bowl, whisk together the reduced pomegranate juice, honey, eggs, vanilla extract, and salt.
5. Pour the pomegranate mixture into the tart crust.
6. Bake for 30-35 minutes, or until the center is set.
7. Allow the tart to cool completely before garnishing with fresh pomegranate seeds.
8. Slice and serve your Pomegranate and Honey Tart.

Nutrition Facts: Calories: 220 | Total Fat: 11g | Cholesterol: 70mg | Sodium: 160mg | Carbohydrates: 29g

Turkish Rice Pudding (Sütlaç)

Prep Time: 10 minutes | Cook Time: 1 hour | Serves: 6

Ingredients:
• 1 cup short-grain rice
• 4 cups milk
• 1 cup sugar
• 1 teaspoon vanilla extract
• A pinch of salt
• Ground cinnamon for garnish

Instructions:
1. Rinse the rice under cold water until the water runs clear.
2. In a saucepan, combine the rice, milk, and sugar.
3. Bring to a boil, then reduce the heat and simmer for 45-50 minutes, stirring occasionally, until the rice is tender and the pudding is thickened.
4. Stir in the vanilla extract and salt.
5. Divide the pudding among serving bowls or glasses.
6. Allow to cool to room temperature, then refrigerate until chilled.
7. Before serving, sprinkle with ground cinnamon.
8. Enjoy your Turkish Rice Pudding!

Nutrition Facts: Calories: 260 | Total Fat: 3g | Cholesterol: 10mg | Sodium: 85mg | Carbohydrates: 53g

Greek Almond and Orange Cake

Prep Time: 20 minutes | Cook Time: 45 minutes | Serves: 8

Ingredients:
• 2 oranges
• 1 1/2 cups ground almonds
• 3/4 cup granulated sugar
• 1 teaspoon baking powder
• 4 large eggs
• Powdered sugar for dusting (optional)

Instructions:
1. Preheat your oven to 350°F (175°C). Grease and line an 8-inch (20 cm) round cake tin.
2. Wash the oranges and place them in a pot. Cover with water and bring to a boil. Reduce heat and simmer for 2 hours.

3. Drain and allow the oranges to cool, then cut them in half and remove any seeds. Blend the oranges, including the peel, in a food processor until smooth.
4. In a bowl, combine the ground almonds, granulated sugar, and baking powder.
5. Add the eggs and blended oranges to the dry ingredients, mixing until well combined.
6. Pour the batter into the prepared tin and bake for 45 minutes, or until a skewer inserted into the center comes out clean.
7. Allow the cake to cool in the tin for 10 minutes, then turn out onto a wire rack to cool completely.
8. Dust with powdered sugar before serving, if desired.

Nutrition Facts: Calories: 270 | Total Fat: 14g | Cholesterol: 93mg | Sodium: 38mg | Carbohydrates: 30g | Dietary Fiber: 3g

Mediterranean Fig and Walnut Baklava

Prep Time: 30 minutes | Cook Time: 50 minutes | Serves: 12

Ingredients:
• 1 package (16 oz) phyllo dough, thawed
• 2 cups walnuts, chopped
• 1 cup dried figs, finely chopped
• 1 teaspoon ground cinnamon
• 1 cup unsalted butter, melted
• 1 cup granulated sugar
• 1 cup water
• 1/2 cup honey
• 1 teaspoon vanilla extract

Instructions:
1. Preheat your oven to 350°F (175°C).
2. In a bowl, combine the walnuts, figs, and cinnamon.
3. Brush a 9x13 inch baking pan with melted butter. Place one sheet of phyllo in the pan, brush with more butter, and repeat until you have 8 sheets layered.
4. Sprinkle a thin layer of the walnut mixture over the phyllo.
5. Continue layering and buttering the phyllo, then adding the walnut mixture, until all the filling is used, ending with a final layer of 8 sheets of phyllo.
6. Using a sharp knife, cut the baklava into diamond or square shapes.
7. Bake for 50 minutes, or until the baklava is golden and crisp.
8. While the baklava is baking, make the syrup: In a saucepan, combine the sugar, water, honey, and vanilla. Bring to a boil, then reduce heat and simmer for 10 minutes.
9. Remove the baklava from the oven and immediately pour the syrup over it.
10. Allow the baklava to cool completely before serving.

Nutrition Facts: Calories: 450 | Total Fat: 26g | Cholesterol: 40mg | Sodium: 170mg | Carbohydrates: 52g

Pistachio and Olive Oil Cake

Prep Time: 15 minutes | Cook Time: 35 minutes | Serves: 8

Ingredients:
- 1 cup all-purpose flour
- 1/2 cup ground pistachios
- 1 1/2 teaspoons baking powder
- 1/4 teaspoon salt
- 3/4 cup granulated sugar
- 3 large eggs
- 1/2 cup olive oil
- 1/2 cup milk
- 1 teaspoon vanilla extract

Instructions:
1. Preheat your oven to 350°F (175°C). Grease and flour an 8-inch (20 cm) round cake tin.
2. In a bowl, combine the flour, ground pistachios, baking powder, and salt.
3. In another bowl, beat together the sugar and eggs until light and fluffy.
4. Gradually add the olive oil, beating continuously.
5. Add the flour mixture in three additions, alternating with the milk, beginning and ending with the flour. Stir in the vanilla extract.
6. Pour the batter into the prepared tin and smooth the top.
7. Bake for 35 minutes, or until a skewer inserted into the center comes out clean.
8. Allow the cake to cool in the tin for 10 minutes, then turn out onto a wire rack to cool completely.

Nutrition Facts: Calories: 330 | Total Fat: 19g | Cholesterol: 70mg | Sodium: 120mg | Carbohydrates: 36g

Rose Water and Berry Gelato

Prep Time: 10 minutes | Cook Time: 10 minutes | Serves: 6

Ingredients:
- 2 cups mixed berries (such as strawberries, raspberries, and blueberries)
- 3/4 cup granulated sugar
- 2 cups whole milk
- 1 cup heavy cream
- 1 tablespoon rose water
- 1 teaspoon vanilla extract

Instructions:
1. In a saucepan, combine the berries and sugar. Cook over medium heat until the berries release their juices and the sugar dissolves.
2. Blend the berry mixture until smooth, then strain through a fine-mesh sieve to remove the seeds.
3. In a bowl, combine the strained berry mixture, milk, cream, rose water, and vanilla extract.
4. Chill the mixture in the refrigerator for at least 2 hours, or until very cold.
5. Churn the mixture in an ice cream maker according to the manufacturer's instructions.
6. Transfer the gelato to an airtight container and freeze until firm, about 2 hours.
7. Serve the Rose Water and Berry Gelato.

Nutrition Facts: Calories: 280 | Total Fat: 16g | Cholesterol: 55mg | Sodium: 40mg | Carbohydrates: 31g

Turkish Semolina Helva

Prep Time: 5 minutes | Cook Time: 20 minutes | Serves: 6

Ingredients:
- 1 cup semolina
- 1/2 cup unsalted butter
- 1 cup granulated sugar
- 1 1/2 cups water
- 1 teaspoon vanilla extract
- Ground cinnamon for garnish (optional)

Instructions:
1. In a saucepan, melt the butter over medium heat.
2. Add the semolina and cook, stirring constantly, until it is golden brown, about 5 minutes.
3. In another saucepan, combine the sugar and water. Bring to a boil, then reduce heat and simmer until the sugar is dissolved.
4. Gradually add the sugar syrup to the semolina, stirring constantly. Be careful as it may splatter.
5. Continue to cook, stirring, until the mixture thickens and pulls away from the sides of the pan, about 10 minutes.
6. Stir in the vanilla extract.
7. Transfer the helva to a serving dish or individual bowls. Allow to cool slightly before serving.
8. Sprinkle with ground cinnamon, if using.

Nutrition Facts: Calories: 340 | Total Fat: 16g | Cholesterol: 40mg | Sodium: 5mg | Carbohydrates: 46g

Greek Yogurt Parfait with Fresh Fruit

Prep Time: 10 minutes | Serves: 4

Ingredients:
- 2 cups Greek yogurt
- 1 cup granola
- 2 cups mixed fresh fruits (berries, kiwi, banana slices, etc.)
- 2 tablespoons honey
- Fresh mint leaves for garnish (optional)

Instructions:
1. In serving glasses or bowls, start by layering 2 tablespoons of Greek yogurt at the bottom.
2. Add a layer of granola followed by a layer of mixed fresh fruits.
3. Repeat the layers until the glasses are filled, ending with a fruit layer on top.
4. Drizzle honey over the fruit.
5. Garnish with fresh mint leaves if desired.
6. Serve immediately or refrigerate until ready to serve.

Nutrition Facts: Calories: 230 | Total Fat: 6g | Saturated Fat: 0.5g | Cholesterol: 5mg | Sodium: 60mg | Carbohydrates: 36g | Dietary Fiber: 4g | Sugars: 22g | Protein: 12g

Mediterranean Citrus Tart

Prep Time: 30 minutes | Cook Time: 40 minutes | Serves: 8

Ingredients:
- 1 pre-baked tart shell (9 inches)
- 1/2 cup granulated sugar
- 3 large eggs
- 1/2 cup fresh citrus juice (orange, lemon, grapefruit mix)
- Zest of 1 lemon
- Zest of 1 orange
- 1/4 cup melted unsalted butter
- Powdered sugar for dusting (optional)

Instructions:
1. Preheat your oven to 350°F (175°C).
2. In a mixing bowl, whisk together the sugar and eggs until light and fluffy.
3. Add the citrus juice, lemon zest, orange zest, and melted butter; mix well.
4. Pour the citrus mixture into the pre-baked tart shell.
5. Bake for 30-40 minutes or until the filling is set.
6. Allow the tart to cool completely before serving.
7. Dust with powdered sugar before serving, if desired.

Nutrition Facts: Calories: 180 | Total Fat: 9g | Cholesterol: 75mg | Sodium: 50mg | Total Carbohydrates: 22g | Sugars: 14g | Protein: 3g

Lavender and Honey Madeleines

Prep Time: 15 minutes | Cook Time: 10 minutes | Serves: 12

Ingredients:
- 2 large eggs
- 1/2 cup granulated sugar
- 1 cup all-purpose flour
- 1/2 teaspoon baking powder
- 1/4 teaspoon salt
- 1/2 cup unsalted butter, melted and cooled
- 2 tablespoons honey
- 1 teaspoon lavender flowers, finely ground
- Powdered sugar for dusting (optional)

Instructions:
1. Preheat your oven to 375°F (190°C) and grease a madeleine pan.
2. In a mixing bowl, beat the eggs and sugar together until thick and pale.
3. Sift in the flour, baking powder, and salt; gently fold into the egg mixture.
4. Add the melted butter, honey, and ground lavender; fold until just combined.
5. Spoon the batter into the madeleine molds, filling each about 3/4 full.
6. Bake for 8-10 minutes or until the edges are golden brown and the centers spring back when lightly touched.
7. Remove from the oven and immediately turn out onto a wire rack to cool.
8. Dust with powdered sugar before serving, if desired.

Nutrition Facts: Calories: 140 | Total Fat: 8g

| Cholesterol: 45mg | Sodium: 65mg | Total Carbohydrates: 16g

Pomegranate Panna Cotta

Prep Time: 15 minutes | Cook Time: 5 minutes | Serves: 6

Ingredients:
- 2 cups heavy cream
- 1/2 cup granulated sugar
- 1 teaspoon vanilla extract
- 2 1/4 teaspoons gelatin powder
- 3 tablespoons cold water
- 1 cup pomegranate juice
- Pomegranate seeds for garnish (optional)

Instructions:
1. In a saucepan, combine the heavy cream and sugar. Heat over medium heat until the sugar is dissolved and the mixture is hot.
2. Remove from heat and stir in the vanilla extract.
3. In a small bowl, sprinkle the gelatin over the cold water; let it sit for 1-2 minutes.
4. Add the gelatin mixture to the hot cream mixture; stir until the gelatin is completely dissolved.
5. Stir in the pomegranate juice.
6. Pour the mixture into ramekins or glasses; refrigerate for at least 4 hours or until set.
7. Garnish with pomegranate seeds before serving, if desired.

Nutrition Facts: Calories: 340 | Total Fat: 28g | Cholesterol: 105mg | Sodium: 30mg | Total Carbohydrates: 22g

Baklava Bites

Prep Time: 20 minutes | Cook Time: 20 minutes | Serves: 24

Ingredients:
- 1 package phyllo dough, thawed
- 1 cup mixed nuts (walnuts, pistachios, almonds), finely chopped
- 1/2 cup unsalted butter, melted
- 1 teaspoon ground cinnamon
- 1 cup granulated sugar
- 1/2 cup water
- 1/2 cup honey
- 1 teaspoon vanilla extract

Instructions:
1. Preheat your oven to 350°F (175°C) and grease a mini muffin pan.
2. Cut the phyllo dough into squares that will fit into the mini muffin cups.
3. Place one square of phyllo in each cup, brush with melted butter, and repeat, layering and buttering each square, until you have 6 layers in each cup.
4. Mix the chopped nuts with the ground cinnamon and sprinkle a small amount into each cup.
5. Bake for 15-20 minutes or until golden brown.
6. While the baklava is baking, make the syrup: In a saucepan, combine the sugar, water, honey, and vanilla extract. Bring to a boil, then reduce heat and simmer for

10 minutes.
7. Remove the baklava from the oven and immediately pour the syrup over each cup.
8. Allow to cool in the pan before serving.

Nutrition Facts: Calories: 140 | Total Fat: 7g | Saturated Fat: 3g | Cholesterol: 10mg | Sodium: 35mg | Total Carbohydrates: 19g | Dietary Fiber: 1g | Sugars: 13g | Protein: 2g

Greek Yogurt and Cherry Clafoutis

Prep Time: 10 minutes | **Cook Time:** 35 minutes | **Serves:** 8

Ingredients:
- 2 cups fresh or frozen cherries, pitted
- 3 large eggs
- 1 cup Greek yogurt
- 1/2 cup granulated sugar
- 1 teaspoon vanilla extract
- 1/2 cup all-purpose flour
- A pinch of salt
- Powdered sugar for dusting (optional)

Instructions:
1. Preheat your oven to 375°F (190°C). Grease a 9-inch round baking dish.
2. Spread the cherries in an even layer in the prepared baking dish.
3. In a mixing bowl, whisk together the eggs, Greek yogurt, sugar, and vanilla extract until smooth.
4. Sift in the flour and salt, then whisk until just combined.
5. Pour the batter over the cherries.
6. Bake for 35-40 minutes, or until the clafoutis is set and golden brown.
7. Allow to cool for 10 minutes before serving.
8. Dust with powdered sugar before serving, if desired.

Nutrition Facts: Calories: 140 | Total Fat: 2g | Saturated Fat: 1g | Cholesterol: 70mg | Sodium: 40mg | Total Carbohydrates: 26g | Dietary Fiber: 1g | Sugars: 18g | Protein: 5g

Orange Blossom Almond Cake

Prep Time: 15 minutes | **Cook Time:** 50 minutes | **Serves:** 10

Ingredients:
- 2 cups almond flour
- 3/4 cup granulated sugar
- 1 teaspoon baking powder
- 1/2 cup unsalted butter, melted
- 4 large eggs
- 2 tablespoons orange blossom water
- Zest of 1 orange
- Powdered sugar for dusting (optional)

Instructions:
1. Preheat your oven to 350°F (175°C). Grease a 9-inch round cake pan.
2. In a mixing bowl, combine the almond flour, sugar, and baking powder.
3. Add the melted butter, eggs, orange blossom water,

and orange zest. Mix until well combined.
4. Pour the batter into the prepared cake pan.
5. Bake for 45-50 minutes, or until a toothpick inserted into the center comes out clean.
6. Allow the cake to cool in the pan for 10 minutes, then transfer to a wire rack to cool completely.
7. Dust with powdered sugar before serving, if desired.

Nutrition Facts: Calories: 290 | Total Fat: 23g | Saturated Fat: 7g | Cholesterol: 90mg | Sodium: 40mg | Total Carbohydrates: 17g | Dietary Fiber: 3g | Sugars: 13g | Protein: 8g

Mediterranean Apricot and Almond Tart

Prep Time: 20 minutes | **Cook Time:** 40 minutes | **Serves:** 8

Ingredients:
- 1 pre-baked tart shell (9 inches)
- 1 cup dried apricots, chopped
- 1 cup almond flour
- 1/2 cup granulated sugar
- 1/2 cup unsalted butter, softened
- 3 large eggs
- 1 teaspoon vanilla extract
- Sliced almonds for garnish (optional)

Instructions:
1. Preheat your oven to 350°F (175°C).
2. Spread the chopped apricots evenly over the bottom of the tart shell.
3. In a mixing bowl, combine the almond flour, sugar, butter, eggs, and vanilla extract. Mix until smooth.
4. Pour the almond mixture over the apricots.
5. Bake for 35-40 minutes, or until the tart is set and golden brown.
6. Allow to cool before serving.
7. Garnish with sliced almonds before serving, if desired.

Nutrition Facts: Calories: 320 | Total Fat: 20g | Saturated Fat: 9g | Cholesterol: 90mg | Sodium: 40mg | Total Carbohydrates: 29g | Dietary Fiber: 3g | Sugars: 19g | Protein: 7g

Lemon and Olive Oil Sorbet

Prep Time: 10 minutes | **Cook Time:** 5 minutes | **Serves:** 6

Ingredients:
- 1 cup granulated sugar
- 1 cup water
- Zest of 2 lemons
- 3/4 cup fresh lemon juice
- 1/4 cup extra virgin olive oil
- Fresh mint leaves for garnish (optional)

Instructions:
1. In a saucepan, combine the sugar, water, and lemon zest. Bring to a boil over medium heat, stirring until the sugar is dissolved.
2. Remove from heat and let cool to room temperature.
3. Strain the mixture into a bowl, discarding the lemon

zest.

4. Stir in the lemon juice and olive oil until well combined.

5. Pour the mixture into an ice cream maker and churn according to the manufacturer's instructions.

6. Transfer the sorbet to a container and freeze until firm, at least 2 hours.

7. Serve garnished with fresh mint leaves, if desired.

Nutrition Facts: Calories: 210 | Total Fat: 5g | Saturated Fat: 1g | Total Carbohydrates: 41g

Turkish Almond and Pistachio Baklava

Prep Time: 30 minutes | Cook Time: 50 minutes | Serves: 20

Ingredients:
- 1 package phyllo dough, thawed
- 1 cup unsalted butter, melted
- 2 cups almonds, finely chopped
- 1 cup pistachios, finely chopped
- 1 teaspoon ground cinnamon
- 1 cup granulated sugar
- 1 cup water
- 1/2 cup honey
- 1 teaspoon vanilla extract
- Juice of half a lemon

Instructions:
1. Preheat your oven to 350°F (175°C).
2. Brush a 9x13-inch baking dish with melted butter.
3. Lay one sheet of phyllo dough in the prepared baking dish, brush with melted butter, and repeat with 8 more sheets.
4. Mix together the almonds, pistachios, and ground cinnamon. Spread a thin layer of the nut mixture over the phyllo dough.
5. Continue layering and buttering phyllo sheets, then adding the nut mixture, until all the nuts are used, finishing with a layer of 10 buttered phyllo sheets.
6. Using a sharp knife, cut the baklava into diamond or square shapes.
7. Bake for 50 minutes, or until the baklava is golden brown and crisp.
8. While the baklava is baking, make the syrup: In a saucepan, combine the sugar, water, honey, vanilla extract, and lemon juice. Bring to a boil, then reduce heat and simmer for 10 minutes.
9. Remove the baklava from the oven and immediately pour the syrup over the hot baklava.
10. Allow to cool completely before serving.

Nutrition Facts: Calories: 290 | Total Fat: 18g | Saturated Fat: 6g | Cholesterol: 15mg | Sodium: 85mg | Total Carbohydrates: 29g | Dietary Fiber: 2g | Sugars: 17g | Protein: 4g

Lavender Creme Brulee

Prep Time: 15 minutes | Cook Time: 40 minutes + 4 hours chilling | Serves: 6

Ingredients:
- 2 cups heavy cream
- 1 tablespoon dried lavender flowers
- 6 large egg yolks
- 1/2 cup granulated sugar, plus more for topping
- 1 teaspoon vanilla extract

Instructions:
1. Preheat your oven to 325°F (160°C).
2. In a saucepan over medium heat, warm the cream until it's hot but not boiling. Remove from heat and add the lavender flowers. Cover and let steep for 10 minutes.
3. Strain the cream through a fine mesh sieve to remove the lavender. Return the cream to the saucepan and reheat until it's hot again.
4. In a mixing bowl, whisk together the egg yolks, sugar, and vanilla extract until well combined.
5. Slowly pour the hot cream into the egg yolk mixture, whisking constantly.
6. Divide the mixture among 6 ramekins. Place the ramekins in a baking dish and fill the dish with hot water until it comes halfway up the sides of the ramekins.
7. Bake for 30-40 minutes, or until the centers are just set.
8. Remove from the oven and let cool to room temperature. Refrigerate for at least 4 hours, or until firm.
9. Before serving, sprinkle each ramekin with a thin layer of sugar. Use a kitchen torch to caramelize the sugar until it's golden brown, serve immediately.

Nutrition Facts: Calories: 375 | Total Fat: 30g | Saturated Fat: 18g | Cholesterol: 260mg | Sodium: 35mg | Total Carbohydrates: 23g

Mediterranean Chocolate and Olive Oil Cake

Prep Time: 15 minutes | Cook Time: 30 minutes | Serves: 8

Ingredients:
- 200g dark chocolate (70% cocoa), chopped
- 3 tablespoons extra virgin olive oil
- 100g granulated sugar
- 3 large eggs, separated
- 1 teaspoon vanilla extract
- 1/2 teaspoon sea salt
- Powdered sugar for dusting (optional)

Instructions:
1. Preheat your oven to 350°F (175°C). Grease and line an 8-inch (20cm) round cake pan.
2. Melt the chocolate in a heatproof bowl over a pot of simmering water. Once melted, remove from heat and whisk in the olive oil. Let cool slightly.
3. In a separate bowl, whisk the egg yolks with half of the sugar until pale and slightly thickened.
4. Gently fold the chocolate mixture into the egg yolks.
5. In another clean, dry bowl, beat the egg whites with a pinch of salt until soft peaks form. Gradually add the

remaining sugar, beating until glossy.
6. Gently fold the egg whites into the chocolate mixture, in three additions, until no white streaks remain.
7. Pour the batter into the prepared pan and smooth the top.
8. Bake for 25-30 minutes, or until a skewer inserted into the center comes out with a few moist crumbs attached.
9. Let cool in the pan for 10 minutes, then turn out onto a wire rack to cool completely.
10. Dust with powdered sugar before serving, if desired.

Nutrition Facts: Calories: 280 | Total Fat: 18g | Saturated Fat: 8g | Cholesterol: 80mg | Sodium: 180mg | Total Carbohydrates: 24g | Dietary Fiber: 3g | Sugars: 18g | Protein: 5g

Greek Walnut Cake (Karidopita)

Prep Time: 20 minutes | Cook Time: 45 minutes | Serves: 10

Ingredients:
• 1 cup all-purpose flour
• 1 teaspoon baking powder
• 1 teaspoon ground cinnamon
• 1/2 teaspoon ground cloves
• 1/4 teaspoon salt
• 1 cup ground walnuts
• 3/4 cup granulated sugar
• 3 large eggs
• 1 teaspoon vanilla extract
• 1/2 cup olive oil
• 1/2 cup milk

Syrup:
• 1 cup granulated sugar
• 1/2 cup water
• 1/2 cup honey
• 1 cinnamon stick
• 3 cloves
• Juice of 1 lemon

Instructions:
1. Preheat your oven to 350°F (175°C). Grease and flour a 9-inch (23cm) round cake pan.
2. In a bowl, combine the flour, baking powder, ground cinnamon, ground cloves, and salt. Set aside.
3. In another bowl, mix together the ground walnuts, sugar, eggs, vanilla extract, olive oil, and milk.
4. Add the dry ingredients to the wet ingredients, stirring just until combined.
5. Pour the batter into the prepared pan and smooth the top.
6. Bake for 45 minutes, or until a toothpick inserted into the center comes out clean.
7. While the cake is baking, make the syrup: Combine all the syrup ingredients in a saucepan and bring to a boil. Reduce heat and simmer for 10 minutes.
8. Remove the cake from the oven and immediately pour the hot syrup over it.
9. Allow the cake to cool completely in the pan before serving.

Nutrition Facts: Calories: 420 | Total Fat: 23g | Saturated Fat: 3g | Cholesterol: 55mg | Sodium: 95mg

| Total Carbohydrates: 49g | Dietary Fiber: 1g | Sugars: 37g | Protein: 6g

Pomegranate and Pistachio Chocolate Bark

Prep Time: 10 minutes | Cook Time: 5 minutes | Serves: 10

Ingredients:
• 200g dark chocolate (70% cocoa), chopped
• 1/2 cup pomegranate arils
• 1/2 cup shelled pistachios, chopped
• A pinch of sea salt

Instructions:
1. Line a baking sheet with parchment paper.
2. Melt the chocolate in a heatproof bowl over a pot of simmering water, stirring until smooth.
3. Pour the melted chocolate onto the prepared baking sheet, spreading it out into a thin layer.
4. Sprinkle the pomegranate arils, pistachios, and sea salt over the chocolate.
5. Place in the refrigerator to set, about 1 hour.
6. Once set, break the chocolate bark into pieces and serve.

Nutrition Facts: Calories: 180 | Total Fat: 12g | Saturated Fat: 6g | Cholesterol: 0mg | Sodium: 20mg | Total Carbohydrates: 17g | Dietary Fiber: 3g | Sugars: 11g | Protein: 3g

Lemon and Almond Olive Oil Cake

Prep Time: 15 minutes | Cook Time: 40 minutes | Serves: 8

Ingredients:
• 1 1/2 cups all-purpose flour
• 2 teaspoons baking powder
• 1/2 teaspoon salt
• 1 cup granulated sugar
• Zest of 2 lemons
• 3/4 cup extra-virgin olive oil
• 2 large eggs
• 1/2 cup almond milk
• 1/2 cup fresh lemon juice
• 1 teaspoon vanilla extract
• 1/2 cup sliced almonds, for topping

Instructions:
1. Preheat your oven to 350°F (175°C). Grease and flour a 9-inch (23cm) round cake pan.
2. In a bowl, whisk together the flour, baking powder, and salt.
3. In another bowl, combine the sugar and lemon zest, rubbing them together with your fingertips to release the oils from the zest.
4. Add the olive oil, eggs, almond milk, lemon juice, and vanilla extract to the sugar mixture, whisking until well combined.
5. Add the dry ingredients to the wet ingredients, stirring just until combined.
6. Pour the batter into the prepared pan, smoothing the top.

7. Sprinkle the sliced almonds over the top of the batter.
8. Bake for 35-40 minutes, or until a toothpick inserted into the center comes out clean.
9. Let cool in the pan for 10 minutes, then turn out onto a wire rack to cool completely.

Nutrition Facts: Calories: 430 | Total Fat: 27g | Saturated Fat: 4g | Cholesterol: 45mg | Sodium: 210mg | Total Carbohydrates: 42g | Dietary Fiber: 1g | Sugars: 24g | Protein: 6g

Turkish Delight Ice Cream

Prep Time: 15 minutes | Cook Time: 5 minutes | Serves: 8

Ingredients:
- 2 cups heavy cream
- 1 cup whole milk
- 3/4 cup granulated sugar
- 1 teaspoon vanilla extract
- 1/2 cup Turkish delight, chopped
- Rose water to taste (optional)

Instructions:
1. In a mixing bowl, combine the heavy cream, whole milk, granulated sugar, and vanilla extract.
2. Whisk until the sugar has fully dissolved into the mixture.
3. Stir in the rose water if using, adjusting to taste.
4. Churn the mixture in an ice cream maker according to the manufacturer's instructions.
5. In the last few minutes of churning, add the chopped Turkish delight, allowing it to mix throughout the ice cream.
6. Transfer the ice cream to a freezer-safe container and freeze until firm, about 2-4 hours.

Nutrition Facts: Calories: 320 | Total Fat: 22g | Saturated Fat: 14g | Cholesterol: 80mg | Sodium: 25mg | Total Carbohydrates: 29g | Sugars: 27g | Protein: 2g

Fig and Honey Cheesecake

Prep Time: 20 minutes | Cook Time: 50 minutes | Serves: 12

Ingredients:
- 1 1/2 cups graham cracker crumbs
- 1/2 cup melted unsalted butter
- 3 cups cream cheese, softened
- 1 cup granulated sugar
- 3 large eggs
- 1/2 cup honey
- 1 teaspoon vanilla extract
- 1 cup dried figs, chopped
- Zest of 1 lemon

Instructions:
1. Preheat your oven to 325°F (160°C). Grease and line a 9-inch (23cm) springform pan.
2. In a bowl, combine the graham cracker crumbs and melted butter, mixing until the crumbs are fully moistened.
3. Press the mixture firmly into the bottom of the prepared pan to form the crust.

4. In a large mixing bowl, beat the cream cheese until smooth and creamy.
5. Add the granulated sugar, eggs, honey, and vanilla extract, beating well after each addition.
6. Stir in the chopped figs and lemon zest.
7. Pour the cream cheese mixture over the prepared crust in the pan.
8. Bake for 50-60 minutes, or until the center is set and the top is lightly browned.
9. Allow the cheesecake to cool in the pan before transferring it to the refrigerator to chill for at least 4 hours.
10. Once chilled, remove from the pan and serve.

Nutrition Facts: Calories: 430 | Total Fat: 27g | Saturated Fat: 15g | Cholesterol: 115mg | Sodium: 260mg | Total Carbohydrates: 42g | Dietary Fiber: 1g | Sugars: 32g | Protein: 6g

Mediterranean Lemon Tart

Prep Time: 20 minutes | Cook Time: 40 minutes | Serves: 8

Ingredients:
- 1 1/4 cups all-purpose flour
- 1/4 cup granulated sugar
- 1/2 cup unsalted butter, cold and cut into pieces
- 1/4 teaspoon salt
- 3 large eggs
- 1 cup granulated sugar
- 1 tablespoon lemon zest
- 1/2 cup fresh lemon juice
- 1/4 cup whole milk
- Powdered sugar for dusting (optional)

Instructions:
1. Preheat your oven to 350°F (175°C). Grease a 9-inch (23cm) tart pan.
2. In a food processor, combine the flour, 1/4 cup sugar, butter, and salt. Pulse until the mixture resembles coarse crumbs.
3. Press the mixture firmly into the bottom and up the sides of the prepared tart pan.
4. Bake the crust for 15 minutes, or until it's lightly golden.
5. In a mixing bowl, whisk together the eggs, 1 cup sugar, lemon zest, lemon juice, and milk.
6. Pour the lemon mixture into the pre-baked crust.
7. Bake for an additional 25 minutes, or until the filling is set.
8. Allow the tart to cool completely before serving. Dust with powdered sugar if desired.

Nutrition Facts: Calories: 300 | Total Fat: 12g | Saturated Fat: 7g | Cholesterol: 95mg | Sodium: 85mg | Total Carbohydrates: 44g | Dietary Fiber: 1g | Sugars: 30g | Protein: 4g

Olive Oil and Orange Cake

Prep Time: 15 minutes | Cook Time: 40 minutes | Serves: 8

Ingredients:
- 1 1/2 cups all-purpose flour

- 2 teaspoons baking powder
- 1/2 teaspoon salt
- 1 cup granulated sugar
- Zest of 2 oranges
- 3/4 cup extra-virgin olive oil
- 3 large eggs
- 1/2 cup fresh orange juice
- 1 teaspoon vanilla extract

Instructions:
1. Preheat your oven to 350°F (175°C). Grease and flour a 9-inch (23cm) round cake pan.
2. In a bowl, whisk together the flour, baking powder, and salt.
3. In another bowl, combine the sugar and orange zest, rubbing them together with your fingertips to release the oils from the zest.
4. Add the olive oil, eggs, orange juice, and vanilla extract to the sugar mixture, whisking until well combined.
5. Add the dry ingredients to the wet ingredients, stirring just until combined.
6. Pour the batter into the prepared pan, smoothing the top.
7. Bake for 35-40 minutes, or until a toothpick inserted into the center comes out clean.
8. Let cool in the pan for 10 minutes, then turn out onto a wire rack to cool completely.

Nutrition Facts: Calories: 400 | Total Fat: 23g | Saturated Fat: 4g | Cholesterol: 70mg | Sodium: 160mg | Total Carbohydrates: 44g | Dietary Fiber: 1g | Sugars: 25g | Protein: 5g

Turkish Apricot and Almond Pudding

Prep Time: 10 minutes | Cook Time: 20 minutes | Serves: 6

Ingredients:
- 1 cup dried apricots, chopped
- 2 cups milk
- 1/2 cup granulated sugar
- 1/4 cup ground almonds
- 2 tablespoons cornstarch
- 1 teaspoon vanilla extract
- Almond flakes and apricot slices for garnish (optional)

Instructions:
1. In a saucepan over medium heat, combine the apricots and milk. Bring to a simmer and cook until the apricots are soft, about 10 minutes.
2. In a bowl, mix the sugar, ground almonds, and cornstarch.
3. Add the almond mixture to the saucepan, stirring constantly until the mixture thickens.
4. Remove from heat and stir in the vanilla extract.
5. Pour the pudding into serving dishes and allow to cool.
6. Refrigerate for at least 2 hours before serving. Garnish with almond flakes and apricot slices if desired.

Nutrition Facts: Calories: 220 | Total Fat: 4g | Saturated Fat: 1g | Cholesterol: 5mg | Sodium: 35mg | Total Carbohydrates: 42g | Dietary Fiber: 2g | Sugars: 37g | Protein: 5g

Lavender and Lemon Cookies

Prep Time: 15 minutes | Cook Time: 12 minutes | Serves: 24 cookies

Ingredients:
- 2 cups all-purpose flour
- 1/2 teaspoon baking powder
- 1/4 teaspoon salt
- 1 cup unsalted butter, softened
- 1 cup granulated sugar
- 1 tablespoon dried lavender buds, finely chopped
- Zest of 1 lemon
- 1 large egg
- 1 teaspoon vanilla extract

Instructions:
1. Preheat your oven to 350°F (175°C) and line a baking sheet with parchment paper.
2. In a bowl, whisk together the flour, baking powder, and salt.
3. In another bowl, cream together the butter, sugar, lavender, and lemon zest until light and fluffy.
4. Beat in the egg and vanilla extract.
5. Gradually add the dry ingredients, mixing until just combined.
6. Drop rounded teaspoons of dough onto the prepared baking sheet.
7. Bake for 10-12 minutes, or until the edges are lightly golden.
8. Cool on the baking sheet for 5 minutes before transferring to a wire rack to cool completely.

Nutrition Facts: Calories: 120 | Total Fat: 7g | Saturated Fat: 4g | Cholesterol: 25mg | Sodium: 25mg | Total Carbohydrates: 14g | Sugars: 7g | Protein: 1g

Mediterranean Berry and Yogurt Tart

Prep Time: 20 minutes | Cook Time: 12 minutes | Chill Time: 2 hours | Serves: 8

Ingredients:
- 1 1/4 cups graham cracker crumbs
- 1/4 cup melted butter
- 2 cups Greek yogurt
- 1/4 cup honey
- 1 teaspoon vanilla extract
- 2 cups mixed berries (strawberries, blueberries, raspberries)
- Fresh mint leaves for garnish (optional)

Instructions:
1. Combine the graham cracker crumbs and melted butter, press into the bottom of a tart pan to form the crust. Bake at 350°F (175°C) for 12 minutes or until set. Let it cool completely.
2. In a bowl, mix together the Greek yogurt, honey, and vanilla extract until smooth.
3. Pour the yogurt mixture over the cooled crust, spreading it evenly.
4. Arrange the mixed berries on top of the yogurt.
5. Chill in the refrigerator for at least 2 hours before

serving.
6. Garnish with fresh mint leaves if using, and serve.

Nutrition Facts: Calories: 200 | Total Fat: 7g | Saturated Fat: 4g | Cholesterol: 15mg | Sodium: 150mg | Total Carbohydrates: 30g | Dietary Fiber: 2g | Sugars: 18g | Protein: 5g

Baklava Ice Cream

Prep Time: 20 minutes | Cook Time: 10 minutes | Freeze Time: 4 hours | Serves: 8

Ingredients:
- 2 cups heavy cream
- 1 cup whole milk
- 3/4 cup honey
- 1 teaspoon vanilla extract
- 1 cup chopped baklava

Instructions:
1. In a mixing bowl, combine the heavy cream, whole milk, honey, and vanilla extract.
2. Whisk until the honey is fully dissolved into the mixture.
3. Churn the mixture in an ice cream maker according to the manufacturer's instructions.
4. In the last few minutes of churning, add the chopped baklava, allowing it to mix throughout the ice cream.
5. Transfer the ice cream to a freezer-safe container and freeze until firm, about 4 hours.

Nutrition Facts: Calories: 350 | Total Fat: 22g | Saturated Fat: 13g | Cholesterol: 80mg | Sodium: 100mg | Total Carbohydrates: 34g | Sugars: 30g | Protein: 3g

Greek Yogurt and Honey Popsicles

Prep Time: 5 minutes | Freeze Time: 4 hours | Serves: 6

Ingredients:
- 2 cups Greek yogurt
- 1/4 cup honey
- 1 teaspoon vanilla extract
- Zest of 1 lemon (optional)

Instructions:
1. In a bowl, mix together the Greek yogurt, honey, vanilla extract, and lemon zest if using.
2. Pour the mixture into popsicle molds, inserting sticks.
3. Freeze for at least 4 hours, or until solid.
4. To serve, run the popsicle mold under warm water to easily remove the popsicles.

Nutrition Facts: Calories: 100 | Total Fat: 1g | Cholesterol: 5mg | Sodium: 35mg | Total Carbohydrates: 14g | Sugars: 13g | Protein: 8g

Lemon and Rosemary Olive Oil Cake

Prep Time: 15 minutes | Cook Time: 40 minutes | Serves: 8

Ingredients:
- 1 3/4 cups all-purpose flour
- 1 teaspoon baking powder
- 1/2 teaspoon salt
- 1 cup granulated sugar
- Zest of 2 lemons
- 3/4 cup extra virgin olive oil
- 4 large eggs
- 1/4 cup fresh lemon juice
- 1 teaspoon vanilla extract
- 2 tablespoons fresh rosemary, finely chopped

Instructions:
1. Preheat the oven to 350°F (175°C). Grease and flour a 9-inch (23 cm) round cake pan.
2. In a bowl, whisk together the flour, baking powder, and salt.
3. In another bowl, combine the sugar and lemon zest, rubbing them together with your fingertips to release the oils.
4. Whisk in the olive oil, eggs, lemon juice, vanilla extract, and rosemary.
5. Add the dry ingredients, stirring just until combined.
6. Pour the batter into the prepared pan and smooth the top.
7. Bake for 35-40 minutes, or until a toothpick inserted into the center comes out clean.
8. Let the cake cool in the pan for 10 minutes, then turn it out onto a wire rack to cool completely.

Nutrition Facts: Calories: 400 | Total Fat: 23g | Saturated Fat: 4g | Cholesterol: 80mg | Sodium: 200mg | Total Carbohydrates: 42g | Dietary Fiber: 1g | Sugars: 25g | Protein: 6g

Turkish Pistachio and Apricot Cake

Prep Time: 15 minutes | Cook Time: 35 minutes | Serves: 8

Ingredients:
- 1 cup all-purpose flour
- 1/2 cup ground pistachios
- 1 teaspoon baking powder
- 1/4 teaspoon salt
- 1/2 cup unsalted butter, softened
- 3/4 cup granulated sugar
- 2 large eggs
- 1 teaspoon vanilla extract
- 1/2 cup milk
- 1/2 cup dried apricots, chopped

Instructions:
1. Preheat the oven to 350°F (175°C). Grease and flour an 8-inch (20 cm) round cake pan.
2. In a bowl, whisk together the flour, ground pistachios, baking powder, and salt.
3. In another bowl, cream the butter and sugar together until light and fluffy.
4. Add the eggs one at a time, beating well after each addition. Stir in the vanilla.
5. Add the flour mixture in three parts, alternating with the milk, beginning and ending with the flour. Mix just until combined.
6. Fold in the chopped apricots.
7. Pour the batter into the prepared pan and smooth the top.

8. Bake for 30-35 minutes, or until a toothpick inserted into the center comes out clean.
9. Allow the cake to cool in the pan for 10 minutes, then turn it out onto a wire rack to cool completely.

Nutrition Facts: Calories: 290 | Total Fat: 14g | Saturated Fat: 7g | Cholesterol: 70mg | Sodium: 105mg | Total Carbohydrates: 37g | Dietary Fiber: 2g | Sugars: 21g | Protein: 5g

Fig and Almond Frangipane Tart

Prep Time: 20 minutes | Cook Time: 40 minutes | Serves: 8

Ingredients:
- 1 pastry crust (store-bought or homemade)
- 1 cup ground almonds
- 1/2 cup granulated sugar
- 1/2 cup unsalted butter, softened
- 2 large eggs
- 1 teaspoon vanilla extract
- 1/4 teaspoon almond extract
- 8-10 fresh figs, halved

Instructions:
1. Preheat the oven to 350°F (175°C). Roll out the pastry crust and fit it into a 9-inch (23 cm) tart pan. Trim any excess dough.
2. In a bowl, combine the ground almonds, sugar, butter, eggs, vanilla extract, and almond extract. Mix until smooth.
3. Spread the almond mixture evenly over the pastry crust.
4. Arrange the fig halves, cut side up, on top of the almond mixture.
5. Bake for 35-40 minutes, or until the filling is set and golden brown.
6. Allow the tart to cool completely before serving.

Nutrition Facts: Calories: 340 | Total Fat: 22g | Saturated Fat: 10g | Cholesterol: 85mg | Sodium: 125mg | Total Carbohydrates: 30g | Dietary Fiber: 3g | Sugars: 16g | Protein: 6g

Mediterranean Orange and Almond Cake

Prep Time: 15 minutes | Cook Time: 45 minutes | Serves: 8

Ingredients:
- 2 oranges
- 1 1/2 cups ground almonds
- 1 cup granulated sugar
- 1 teaspoon baking powder
- 4 large eggs

Instructions:
1. Preheat the oven to 350°F (175°C). Grease and flour an 8-inch (20 cm) round cake pan.
2. Wash the oranges and boil them whole for 2 hours, or until soft. Cool, then cut open, remove the seeds and puree the oranges in a food processor.
3. In a bowl, combine the ground almonds, sugar, and baking powder.

4. Add the eggs and pureed oranges, mixing well.
5. Pour the batter into the prepared pan and bake for 40-45 minutes, or until a toothpick inserted into the center comes out clean.
6. Allow the cake to cool in the pan for 10 minutes, then turn it out onto a wire rack to cool completely.

Nutrition Facts: Calories: 350 | Total Fat: 15g | Saturated Fat: 1.5g | Cholesterol: 90mg | Sodium: 40mg | Total Carbohydrates: 47g | Dietary Fiber: 4g | Sugars: 42g | Protein: 9g

Greek Yogurt with Pomegranate and Pistachios

Prep Time: 5 minutes | Serves: 1

Ingredients:
- 1 cup Greek yogurt
- 1/2 cup pomegranate seeds
- 2 tablespoons shelled pistachios
- 1 tablespoon honey

Instructions:
1. Spoon the Greek yogurt into a bowl or serving dish.
2. Top with the pomegranate seeds and pistachios.
3. Drizzle with honey.
4. Serve immediately and enjoy!

Nutrition Facts: Calories: 280 | Total Fat: 9g | Saturated Fat: 1.5g | Cholesterol: 5mg | Sodium: 60mg | Total Carbohydrates: 36g | Dietary Fiber: 4g | Sugars: 30g | Protein: 17g

Lavender and Honey Ice Cream

Prep Time: 10 minutes | Cook Time: 25 minutes | Serves: 6

Ingredients:
- 2 cups heavy cream
- 1 cup whole milk
- 3/4 cup honey
- 2 tablespoons dried culinary lavender
- 6 large egg yolks

Instructions:
1. In a saucepan, combine the cream, milk, honey, and lavender. Bring to a simmer over medium heat, then remove from heat and let steep for 30 minutes.
2. Strain the mixture through a fine-mesh sieve into a bowl, discarding the lavender.
3. In another bowl, whisk the egg yolks until smooth.
4. Gradually whisk in the strained cream mixture.
5. Return the mixture to the saucepan and cook over medium-low heat, stirring constantly, until it thickens enough to coat the back of a spoon.
6. Strain the custard through a fine-mesh sieve into a bowl, then chill in the refrigerator for at least 4 hours or overnight.
7. Once chilled, churn the mixture in an ice cream maker according to the manufacturer's instructions.
8. Transfer the ice cream to a container and freeze until firm, about 2 hours.

Nutrition Facts: Calories: 380 | Total Fat: 28g | Saturated Fat: 17g | Cholesterol: 220mg | Sodium: 45mg | Total Carbohydrates: 30g | Sugars: 29g | Protein: 5g

The Dirty Dozen and Clean Fifteen

The "Dirty Dozen" and "Clean Fifteen" are part of the EWG's annual report, categorizing fruits and vegetables based on their pesticide residues. The Dirty Dozen includes produce with higher residue levels, while the Clean Fifteen features items with lower levels. These lists, aiding consumer awareness, may change annually due to fluctuating test results.

Dirty Dozen: This list features produce with higher pesticide residues, suggesting consumers opt for organic options to minimize exposure. Common items include strawberries, apples, and spinach.

Clean Fifteen: Conversely, this list highlights fruits and vegetables with lower residue levels, considered safer for those concerned about pesticides, with options like avocados and sweet corn.

It's important to note that pesticide residue levels can vary depending on various factors, including farming practices and the specific source of the produce. The lists are intended to provide guidance to consumers who want to make informed choices about their food purchases.

Appendix 1: The Dirty Dozen and Clean Fifteen 2023

2023 CLEAN FIFTEEN LIST

The fruits and veggies with the least pesticide residues

1	Avocado
2	Sweet Corn
3	Pineapples
4	Onions
5	Papayas
6	Sweet Peas (frozen)
7	Asparagus
8	Honeydew Melon
9	Kiwi
10	Cabbage
11	Mushrooms
12	Mangoes
13	Sweet Potatoes
14	Watermelon
15	Carrots

Out of the tested avocado and sweet corn samples, fewer than 2% displayed any measurable pesticide residues.

Approximately 65% of the samples from the Clean Fifteen category showed no traces of pesticide residues.

2023 DIRTY DOZEN LIST

The fruits and veggies with the most pesticide residues

1	Strawberries
2	Spinach
3	Kale, Collard & Mustard Greens
4	Peaches
5	Pears
6	Nectarines
7	Apples
8	Grapes
9	Bell & Hot Peppers
10	Cherries
11	Blueberries
12	Green Beans

Except for cherries, samples from the Dirty Dozen group displayed traces of over 50 different types of pesticides.

Pesticide residue was found in over 90% of samples of strawberries, apples, cherries, spinach, nectarines, and grapes.

Appendix 2: Measurement Conversion Chart

VOLUME EQUIVALENTS (DRY)

US STANDARD	METRIC (APPROXIMATE)
1/8 teaspoon	0.5 mL
1/4 teaspoon	1 mL
1/2 teaspoon	2 mL
3/4 teaspoon	4 mL
1 teaspoon	5 mL
1 tablespoon	15 mL
1/4 cup	59 mL
1/2 cup	118 mL
3/4 cup	177 mL
1 cup	235 mL
2 cups	475 mL
3 cups	700 mL
4 cups	1 L

VOLUME EQUIVALENTS(LIQUID)

US STANDARD	US STANDARD (OUNCE)	METRIC (APPROXIMATE)
2 tablespoons	1 fl.oz.	30 mL
1/4 cup	2 fl.oz.	60 mL
1/2 cup	4 fl.oz.	120 mL
1 cup	8 fl.oz.	240 mL
1 1/2 cup	12 fl.oz.	355 mL
2 cups or 1 pint	16 fl.oz.	475 mL
4 cups or 1 quart	32 fl.oz.	1 L
1 gallon	128 fl.oz.	4 L

TEMPERATURES EQUIVALENTS

FAHRENHEIT(F)	CELSIUS(C)
225°F	107 °C
250°F	120 °C
275°F	135 °C
300°F	150 °C
325°F	160 °C
350°F	180 °C
375°F	190 °C
400°F	205°C
425°F	220°C
450°F	235 °C
475°F	245 °C
500°F	260 °C

WEIGHT EQUIVALENTS

US STANDARD	METRIC (APPROXIMATE)
1 ounce	28 g
2 ounces	57 g
5 ounces	142 g
10 ounces	284 g
15 ounces	425 g
16 ounces / 1 lb.	454 g
32 ounces / 2 lb.	907 g
2.2 lb.	1kg

Enjoy Your Meal

Index

Made in United States
Troutdale, OR
10/02/2024

23318494R00053